COMMANDING YOUR PROFESSIONAL WORTH

A Systems Approach to Rising Up

Kevin Patrick Randall Downey

Ogham Press   Philadelphia

Published by Ogham Press
Philadelphia

First Edition
ISBN# 979-8-9920491-0-7
Library of Congress Control # 2024924786

Cover Art by Madeline Kennedy

Printed in the United States of America

Dedicated to all the strong women I've had the honor of having in my life-past, present, and future.

Dedicated to my wife, my mothers, my daughters, my sisters, my aunts, my cousins, my heroes, and my friends.

COMMANDING YOUR PROFESSIONAL WORTH

A Systems Approach to Rising Up

Introduction
Who is This Book For?

Regardless of pronoun, ethnicity, race, religion, culture, orientation, or demographic, I welcome you. Whatever your background or life experience, if you feel marginalized or disenfranchised, more than anyone, I want you to succeed.

THE RULES OF THE GAME

Do you feel held back? Are you warming the bench? Are you not being recognized or rewarded equally for your merits? Do you work ten times harder than your counterparts?

It matters little whether you are seeking a job, were hired into a company with a lot of competition, are freshly promoted, or are advocating for a raise. The rules of the game are a constant, and it's a dog-eat-dog shark tank with a bit of road rage mixed in, bringing out the worst in otherwise good people.

In this book, I'll introduce you to a tangible system and process for success, and won't waste time offering advice on how to curry the favor of those who aren't worth recruiting to your side. When you are a master of the rules, outperforming, rising up, and dancing past others based on your merits, capability, and confidence, the competition will worry about you—trying to curry your favor—and not the other way around.

MY INSPIRATION

My mom was a hero, and for a time single-handedly supported all of us-me, my brother, and Kathy, our sixteen-year-old babysitter from down the street who was having trouble at home and moved in with us-all while on welfare and putting herself through college. My mother wanted to be a photographer, which was re-prioritized as a hobby, which she eventually sacrificed as well to continue supporting us. She shouldered the burden of a hundred men. She embodied perseverance, integrity, bravery, and love. She was a fighter.

At that time, she wrote a poem that vividly conveys the pain of her sacrifice...

The Decisions

How to choose a silver lined

Pathway through life...

Or to reap the reward of

fulfilling all dreams

and fantasies.

Which path to follow

On the crossroad of life

Which desire will fill

My heart

With fair weather clouds?

To drift away in my

Little boat and leave

All decisions behind

... Ah yes!

WHAT QUALIFIES ME TO WRITE THIS BOOK?

I love coaching others on how to avoid making common mistakes, how to approach their setbacks, how to ask the right questions, how to navigate their way through the weeds, how to expedite their goals, and catapult their careers.

I've volunteered my career coaching services at job fairs, gave lectures on interview techniques, on crafting winning resumes, cover letters, and directed mock interviews with young graduates. I've also served as a contributing writer to MockQuestions.com, where I've written articles, delivered professional interview and leadership coaching advice to both recruiters and to job seekers, and crafted mock interviews tailored to a specific company or profession. My management career spanned across grocery, healthcare, and the high-end art world.

HOW TO NAVIGATE THIS BOOK

This book follows a linear path, from faking it-to believing it-to making it. Jump to relevant sections based on your career stage. However, there is valuable information throughout the book which you may find useful. This book offers a well-constructed systems process for advancing your career in any direction.

This is a comprehensive guide to discovering, establishing, and commanding your professional worth. This equates to more than just pay. What do you want? Whatever you want can be within your grasp. But this requires a better understanding of what you have to offer, and how to showcase your worth in a way that is professionally impossible to ignore.

We'll begin with guidelines for researching everything about you. You first have to know what you're worth before you can expect anyone else to. We'll define your brand and highlight why you're a rockstar and more. Everything that makes you, you! CAPITALIZED, Underlined, **bold print**, *italicized*!

We will use that information to guide you towards maximizing your potential. We will help you create an outstanding resume, compelling CV, all towards delivering a successful interview. This will then graduate to negotiating your salary, benefits, career trajectory, and any other desirable perk until you are rewarded for your professional worth.

Then we'll cover how to rise up in the company you work for. How to track your progress and prove your worth every step of the way. We'll coach you on how to negotiate a raise with every performance review, and how to set yourself up as a rising star, stakeholder, or indispensable partner.

We'll do this by following an enhanced set of questions, based on Konstantin Stanislavsky's great questions. Stanislavsky was a widely known character actor, director, and producer of the stage. He suggested every actor ask themselves a few questions to better understand the character they were playing. The questions are:

- ✦ *Who are you?*
- ✦ *Where are you?*
- ✦ *Why are you here?*

✦ *Where do you come from?*
✦ *Where are you going?*
✦ *How will you get there?*

In this book, I will build upon those crucial questions which are applicable to all professions. Each profession is a role, and every professional is acting that role. Most professions even dress in the uniform or costume associated with that role. A doctor dresses and acts like a doctor. The same goes for a lawyer or a chef. So, your costume is the embodiment of a professional who is at the top of their game, and we'll help you dress that part.

THIS BOOK IS DIVIDED INTO THREE PARTS

Many of the points covered in section one will be touched upon again in section two, and again in section three.

Part one establishes your professional identity and serves as the foundation for your character and personal brand. We are going to concentrate on helping you *discover your professional worth* in clearly defined terms. And I promise you, as you perform your research on yourself, you'll discover some surprises along the way. You'll be amazed at how many skills and talents you've left on the table.

The second part focuses on *establishing your professional worth*. This spans from positioning yourself as their ideal candidate or target talent, to hitting the ground running after getting your foot in the door.

The third part of this book focuses on how to continue *building upon your professional worth*.

Transitioning from an outsider to insider and establishing yourself as an indispensable team member. It will offer you a step-by-step approach to understanding what you're worth compared to what they can afford to pay you, which thereby increases your value. We'll wrap up with *commanding your professional worth* in negotiable terms.

The aim of this book is to help you present yourself as an indispensable asset worth fighting for, and retaining, regardless of cost. That's the bottom line. This book will help you rise up, and to earn and be rewarded based on your merits and accomplishments alone.

Part One
Discovering Your Professional Worth

Being recognized for your professional worth takes far more than working hard or consistently going the extra mile. It takes more than feeling you are owed recognition for your merits or a higher wage than you're presently earning. It goes beyond what seems fair.

It is, unquestionably, about being able to quantify your worth in a measurable way. Being plugged into your organization's goals is essential. If the organization benefits from paying you more, they will be more inclined to accommodate your requests. In the end, satisfying your needs must align with the organization's best interests.

AN UNEVEN PLAYING FIELD

Making a passive impact isn't the same as putting in the bare minimum. In fact, someone who puts in ten times more work and effort than their peers, while not aggressively drawing attention to the impact they're making, qualifies as a passive impact. And, the fact is, rewarding any employee who's making a passive impact goes against any organization's bottom line.

Someone who seems to be putting in the bare minimum is merely earning their base pay and doesn't merit recognition, acknowledgement, promotion, or an increased salary. So, it matters little whether a person who seems to be doing the bare minimum is actually going above and beyond. In fact, it's even better for an organization's bottom line to squeeze more out of their employees without bearing the cost of rewarding them.

THE UNFAIR IMPACT OF COMPETITION

The most assertive, loudest, and most noticed are frequently the most rewarded. So, to attract more attention to themselves, they need to silence their competition. Gaslighting is commonly employed as a subtler approach. They'll often spend time pointing out others' mistakes to highlight their own attention to detail.

They made a mistake, and luckily, my eagle-eye caught it.

They'll throw other people under the bus to deflect attention from their own shortcomings. Or, they might claim credit for others' successes—commonly suggesting the person they 'helped' wouldn't have succeeded without their assistance, and they likely could not repeat their success without their continued supervision.

Ask for help, and they'll be dismissive, coy, guarded, and only offer the most vague advice, such as...

Just keep asking questions.

Every one of these techniques is designed to keep you, or anyone who doesn't fit into their club, from rising up. When successful, they've established power over you.

How can you compete if you're not a sycophant or an attention-seeking person? The answers lie ahead.

THE OBSTACLES PRESENTED BY AUTHORITY

The manner in which someone exerts their power—or displays their model of leadership—typically mirrors their ego. For example, when an ego-centric individual holds a position of power, they'll often come to expect everyone surrounding them to compete for their attention and approval. So, when someone makes it known they're offended or unimpressed by that leader's behavior, it could backfire.

Take the fine line where an 'innocent' joke crosses the line of appropriateness. That's all it sometimes takes to create an unsafe working environment. An employee who is offended by the joke and doesn't laugh might bruise the joke-teller's ego. Realizing they might face repercussions for their actions, the joke-teller might take measures to discredit and marginalize that employee, spreading misconceptions of who they are, defaming their performance level, setting them up for failure, and thereby compromising their professional worth. This leads to a lack of opportunity for that employee, lack of pay equality, and eventually leads to unjustly discharging them. Now, that's one extreme.

Even well-respected leaders can unintentionally abuse power. It wasn't until the *Me-Too movement* that I realized I may have abused my power back in my management days. You see, after I was promoted into a leadership position, I didn't realize the reason everyone was suddenly laughing at all my jokes was correlated with the power I wielded as a manager. I just thought I hit my stride, thanks to my renewed sense of confidence.

The truth is, I'm not that funny, especially not when I try to be. Suddenly I thought I was so funny, all the time. I was always telling stupid jokes and loved the positive attention. But my ego stood in the way of seeing the truth of my situation. I'm now embarrassed by the jokes I told, and for the people who felt obliged to laugh at them. In essence, this was an abuse of power. Most leaders, regardless of whether it is through intention, will eventually abuse their power, overtly or subtly, consciously or subconsciously.

A strong leader must always be mindful of the effect that wielding power has on those surrounding them, and always be diligently mindful, sensitive, empathetic, and disciplined in their conduct. This applies to you as well, since you are the leader of your professional story.

PERCEPTION IS REALITY

One doesn't have to be in a leadership position to exude power. The key to emanating power is believing in the power you wield, having self-respect, and never relinquishing control over the narrative of your story, your attitude, or your life. You need to always be in control of you.

You see, so much of your professional worth is determined by how others perceive your ability and your potential, and has little to do with your actual skills. Therefore, the seat of your professional power lies in the control you have over your own narrative. Your narrative is contextualized by your circumstances. Your attitude towards your circumstances–that which happens to you–and your response or reaction to your circumstances serves as the control panel for your narrative. The only person ever permitted to operate that control panel is you, and it cannot be influenced by outside actors.

For example, let's say someone worked at a job where a peer undermined their efforts and marginalized them. Later, that peer was promoted into a position of authority. Once there, that peer abused their power, and created a toxic work experience.

If that person decided to leave their job for those reasons, they'll be presenting themself as someone who lives their life as a victim, and poses the risk of creating interpersonal issues if hired.

Let's imagine the same person decides to find a job elsewhere because the previous workplace lacked equal opportunity, failed to align with their values, and rewarded favoritism instead of merit. So, they decided to dedicate their time to ensuring the next company they'd work with will meet their expectations, and present the opportunities for advancement they are avidly pursuing. They don't live as a victim. Rather, they held onto their power and took ownership of their career.

Both of these narratives sincerely depict their experience. The only difference is their perception of their given reality, and the attitude they use to convey it. It is through the presentation of their perception that they retain control of how others perceive them, shaping their reality. This is the core philosophy of this book. It is about how you choose to present yourself, throughout your career, from job hunting, to negotiating your starting salary, to proving yourself at work and gaining recognition, to negotiating a raise or promotion.

THE POWER OF PROPAGANDA

Now, the word victim needs to be contextualized here. Anyone can become a victim of crime, sexual harassment, or discrimination, all of which are traumatic experiences. The healing process for such traumas can span years or a lifetime. But when it comes to controlling your narrative and controlling the perception of your professional worth, it is important to recognize the word victim can have multiple connotations.

There is a difference between being a victim of something and going through life as a victim. Those who live as victims have no power and constantly feel victimized. Such a person gets knocked down and stays down. Professionally speaking, this is the definition of failure. Whereas getting up after being knocked down transforms someone from victim to survivor. This person is both a success story and a role model.

Sexual harassment and workplace intimidation can take a variety of forms. These events are not only painful but also traumatic, and often enduring. They can carry a stigma with them, and can even stand in the way of a person finding another job.

Victims are often viewed as having a 'high risk of liability'. You see, most organizations will evaluate a candidate's previous experience and work history as an indicator of their future failure or future success. And, again, perception is reality. Period.

So, if a highly skilled professional advertises that they left their job because of a sexual harassment case that ended in a lawsuit, that recruiter may take pause and consider whether hiring them could pose a risk. That recruiter may fill in the blanks of their narrative.

There's always two sides to the story, they might think. They might wonder if they falsely accused someone of sexual harassment just to fund a frivolous lawsuit. They might question if it was blown out of proportion due to a misunderstanding. These misguided perceptions are the result of a long history of societal propaganda.

Let's quickly define propaganda here. Propaganda, according to the Oxford dictionary, means "information, especially of a biased or misleading nature, used to promote or publicize a particular political cause or point of view." So, by oversharing why they're leaving that employer, they lost their power as well as their control over their narrative.

Is this wrong? Unarguably. But your trauma is none of their business. Remember, that recruiter or hiring authority is not your friend until they prove otherwise. So do not confide in them. Remain boundaried and tell them only what they need to hear. You want to inform them why you are the right person for the job. So communicate that message. Filter out every and any reason that rationalizes bias. Maintain control of your own narrative.

So, model your brand, with your own propaganda, in such a way that advertises your professional worth. And this can be done passively, according to your own nature, without betraying your own ideals. Hint–it will begin with creating an endless number of extremely organized lists. That's where this next section begins. The exercises suggested in this book are all about creating new disciplined habits while shifting your lens to a more strategic narrative.

THE KEY QUESTIONS

Define who you are and everything you have to offer as a professional. Most importantly, this includes everything that fuels your professional drive and growth. This is the path to establishing what you want. The secret to answering these questions depends on you and your character. It requires self-awareness and aligning how you perceive yourself with how others perceive you. It also helps to be honest with yourself about what you want before you draw perimeters around it.

Throughout the first section of this book, you will answer several key questions.

✦ Who am I?
✦ Where am I?
✦ Why am I here?
✦ Where do I come from?
✦ What am I worth?
✦ What do I want?
✦ Where am I going?
✦ What am I up against?
✦ Am I ready to do what it takes to get there?

These questions will help you better understand yourself. Defining who you are will make you more capable of speaking to your character. It will aid you in being able to articulate the time and place you are in your career and your purpose–goals, motives, and the circumstances that led you here. As you answer these questions, you'll be better positioned to persuade others towards your aims, while helping them understand that giving you what you want is in their best interests.

Remember, if you can't identify your worth, no one will do it for you.

Throughout chapters one, two, and three, we will cover how to research who you are and what you have to offer. We'll detail how to unravel every facet of your hidden potential. We'll cover how to start looking at yourself as a highly valued professional and an innovator and leader in your field. Then we'll help you discover your professional worth and how to build upon it.

You have a lot to offer, more than you realize, and you'll be amazed by what you discover as you continue through this book. It will help pave the way to tapping into your potential while positioning yourself as everyone's target talent. We're going to advertise, with greater confidence, everything you have to offer, regardless of whether you're starting out in your career or getting ready to negotiate that corner office, a new title, and your well-deserved raise.

Chapter 1
What Are You Worth & Why Are You Here?

WHO ARE YOU AS A PROFESSIONAL?

There's an etiquette, and a choreographed approach to discovering your professional worth. The better you know and understand yourself, the more empathetic and self-forgiving you'll be.

I can't tell you the number of hard-working professionals I've met over the years who took pride in thinking of themselves as a ninjas. But this is not the way to establish your professional worth. Ninjas are secretive, unseen, and anonymous. A ninja specializes in stealth, espionage, and unconventional warfare, with training in infiltration and disguise.

Rather, a better way to think of yourself is as a samurai. A samurai is someone who has disciplined training in traditional martial arts, swordsmanship, archery, and horseback riding. Also, 50% of all samurai were women. A samurai commands something more than fear. A samurai commands respect. And the first rule as a samurai is knowing thyself. Before you can expect anyone else to know what you are worth, it is up to you to determine and define this yourself. And you have to believe it.

If you've felt marginalized and not taken seriously, you may have convinced yourself you will never have a fair chance. But there are ways to turn the tables and shift the odds to your favor. You first have to rid yourself of self-doubt.

'All battles are first won or lost in the mind.'
- Joan of Arc

Insecurity is an inner battle that must be won, and I am about to reveal what you need to win that battle. The greatest battles are those won without a single casualty. Then, once that battlefield is cleared and inner peace is restored, it's time to strategically pick your battles.

For some out there, this may seem daunting, but it isn't as overwhelming as you'd think. It all starts with regaining sight of what your peers value you for, every positive trait, talent, gift, or skill, and how to advertise your worth. It begins by doing your research on yourself and documenting every finding! Document every significant accomplishment as you continue to self-evaluate.

How far have you come and how hard have you worked to get to where you are standing? How has everything you've learned and experienced informed your decisions until this point? Honestly determine what you are capable of, and how practiced and ready you are to step outside of your comfort zone. Are you ready to take on the challenges ahead of you? Are you looking forward to the hard work to come?

So, you need to establish who you are as a professional. Not only your sense of morality, but your performance standard. The structural integrity of your character centers on your attitude and emotional intelligence, and whether your intellect or your emotions govern your conduct in a professional setting. By answering these questions, you'll better equip yourself to map out your career journey and determine your current experience level.

YOUR CURRICULUM VITAE

People often confuse their resume with their CV. But they are as distinct from each other as your career plan is from your cover letter. So, think of your curriculum vitae (CV) as a detailed overview of your entire professional journey, your accomplishments, skills, and experience.

Candidates who create CVs up to ten pages long for submission are primarily those in academic or research positions. Accomplished career artists as well. However, candidates across most other industries rarely find occasion to submit a CV so extensive, and their materials are reserved to resumes and cover letters. However, no career-minded professional should limit their materials to such, regardless of industry. It doesn't matter if you're pursuing a career with a company, corporation, non-profit, or foundation. You want to keep all of your materials up to date. These should all include your CV, career goals, your brand, your bio, your cover letter, resume, and other materials, which we'll discuss in the ensuing chapters.

Having said that, you'll want to keep your CV on hand and keep it regularly updated. This document will aid you in customizing any resume and cover letter to any opportunity. It will also keep all of your skill sets and accomplishments fresh in your mind and ready to draw from when asked about any topic in an interview or when that skill is required in a time of need.

So, let's start by compiling the most comprehensive CV you've ever had or refreshing your CV if you already have one.

PUTTING YOUR SKILLS TO WORK

It's time to put your organizational techniques into practice. Think about the systems and processes you've relied upon in the past and use whatever method works best for you, whether it is a spreadsheet or a notepad.

Start by creating categories for every skill you've acquired, whether fresh in your mind, forgotten, or taken for granted. Include the organization where you picked up the skill and its chronology, whether at university or at your first or your most recent job.

Write down all your strengths, every time you exemplified leadership potential, the times you thrived, and when you went above and beyond. Even include every nice thing your coworkers have said about you. Continue to research who you are, what you offer, and how you look at yourself as a professional. Catalog every growth lesson learned, professional developments, and accomplishments.

Detail how you navigate your work. For example, if you have a method or standard operating procedures which you implement to perform at your best, there is probably a name for your approach. Find that out so that you can label it and advertise it as a skill.

Whether you're just starting your career or have a decade of experience doesn't matter. The aim here is to shift your mindset to forward-thinking and tapping into your self-discovery. You can be right out of college or in between jobs. You can be burnt out or questioning your next move. This all starts with doing your homework, which entails extensive research on the one subject you have more knowledge of than anyone: you.

Lastly, create another section to your CV where you can catalogue in shorthand every major challenge you've faced, every problem you've solved when you didn't have the answers or the tools to do so, every calculated risk you've taken, every setback and failure, and what you learned from each situation and how you grew, persevered, and promoted the bottom line of the team. Avoid any situations where you were more of a liability than an asset. Rather, list those that showcase rapid growth or the ability to stay cool under pressure or in high-stakes situations. This will help you answer some of the trickiest questions you'll face in future interviews with confidence and swagger.

WHERE TO LOOK

Dig through all of your old records, whether previous roles you've held in your company or previous jobs you've had. It is time to excavate. It doesn't matter if it was the last company you worked for or that summer job in college. Dig out every piece of paper you still have or every digital file you saved. As long as it follows your professional journey, related to your current career path or not, it's relevant. Every job you've had and every skill you've learned holds value here. Find old, outdated resumes and current ones. Go as far back as you can. That construction job when you were twelve or the puppy-sitting you did for your neighbor—it all counts.

Revisit training manuals and onboarding paperwork. Pour through old performance reviews. Comb through every resume you've ever had, workplace bulletins, write-ups, materials you used to manage a project, and even phone numbers of coworkers with whom you connected. Think of every item that triggers a memory of a skill you learned, big or microscopic, and what you learned from it, and any tricks, tips, and training tools which aided in being the best version of you today. Write everything down.

If you helped a coworker learn something new, you're a mentor. If you stepped up to learn something new outside of your comfort zone when your manager asked for volunteers, you're a leader. When you helped deliver your team to success, but didn't claim their success was your own, you saw the big picture and were a loyal and trusted team captain.

Everything counts. It could be something a previous supervisor emphasized or a complementary observation they made about you that you didn't take seriously because it felt patronizing. Or, that obscure strength you forgot about, or didn't consider noteworthy at the time, which now suddenly seems relevant and holds value.

Create piles of paperwork, make folders on your desktop, and write down every responsibility you've ever held, every task you learned or performed, and how many people you trained on those same tasks. Pretty soon, your database on your professional self will take shape. Dive in and get started, and keep adding to it. Make lists and update and organize those lists.

Don't cut any corners and keep at it until you are absolutely sure you've exhausted every avenue.

MENTALLY WALK THE PERIMETER OF EVERY JOB

As an exercise, imagine you are walking into work, whether it was your first job or your current job. Record every step of your day, every task and routine, from the moment you arrive at work until you leave. Start by imagining you are entering the building and are making sure everything is usual or in the right place. Unlock the safe, turn on the computers. Check the schedule. Shoot off emails.... Take in every detail.

Now let's examine every bullet point. If you were entrusted with the keys to the building, or the combo to the safe, you held the responsibility of large cash handling and being a keyholder. Definitely worthy of listing on your CV–and on your resume for relevant positions. This means they trusted you to ensure the company's assets were secure and protected. It also means you take pride in your workplace. Now, when you arrived to work early, did you touch base with everyone you work with, greeting them first thing? This communicates strong time management skills (arriving early), strong interpersonal skills (performing check-ins with each member of your team), and strong communication skills. Combined, they suggest leadership potential.

Already that seems like a lot, and we've barely scratched the surface of what you do in a day. That's just the first five minutes. This is the whole point of this exercise. When you document everything you do, how you put your skills to work, and the knowledge and experience you've accrued, you can describe in measurable ways what makes you unique. Even a thank you note or compliment from a teammate you forgot about can hold value here. Dig into your professional past and go down the rabbit hole until you are swimming in more information than you know what to do with.

You are creating a database for exploring who you are as a professional. It is easy to take yourself for granted and not clearly see in yourself what others see in you. Being more self-aware increases your EQ, and others will trust you more.

THE FOUNDATION OF YOUR WORTH

Those of you who feel self-assured in knowing who you are may wonder what's the point of this exercise? The point is, there is a likelihood you've left selling points on the table all along. If they were fresh in your mind, they could have increased your worth, and everything counts. This will help you align yourself with what a company is seeking. You'll more adeptly fit the mold of their ideal employee. Or better yet, you'll break the mold.

This will assist you in better defining skills that you may have overlooked but would be highly valued for in a future role. Such as how you were a key holder to the building you worked at. That's not something anyone and everyone is entrusted with. And being able to speak to how trusted you are by your superiors, in actionable terms, instantly increases your perceived experience.

For some, this exercise may feel like a chore. For others, it's exciting and fun. This all depends on your personality. But building an arsenal for commanding your professional worth takes work. And you can't do it without a strong foundation. Ultimately, we are laying the foundation for your narrative and who you are as a career-minded professional.

If you can't identify your worth,
no one will do it for you.

In any interview, you'll be asked several questions, such as how you get along with your teammates, or how they might describe you. This exercise will prepare you for those questions. Just by having compiled these research materials and having organized them in advance, you'll be able to showcase the full breadth of your professional experience at the drop of a hat.

So this is a great time to hone in on your organizational skills, and the systematic approach you take with your work. Put your attention to detail to the test. Identify everything you've ever done as a professional. Your CV is your database for customizing future resumes to potential employers.

It will also help you develop a deeper sense of self-awareness, and how to communicate with others. And, self-awareness equates to emotional intelligence, which can help you rise up to the top of the pile, deliver a great interview, and thereby increase your professional worth.

ORGANIZE YOUR DATABASE

Be honest, transparent, and realistic when it comes to your experience level. Don't self-aggrandize your accomplishments and don't sell yourself short either. Just be true and genuinely be yourself. You are your own brand, so stay on-brand. The second you go against the flow of who you are, you lose what makes you unique. It's like singing the song that is you, purposely out of key. It will always backfire and you'll trip over your own feet instead of dancing to the finish line. So, be true to yourself.

This will help you with the next step, where you'll classify these subcategories of skills into two main classifications. Your hard skills and your soft skills.

Hard skills are easy to quantify. These are specific to your background, education, and job experience, which can have a wide range. These things, easily taught and learned, demonstrate your aptitude and intelligence. Such as...

✦ Computer Skills
✦ Accounting skills
✦ Administrative Skills
✦ Grant Writing
✦ Trade Skills
✦ High-End Skills which Require Training and Certifications

Soft skills are harder to quantify. These are things which fall under your smarts, wisdom, or common sense. But, as I always say, common sense isn't all that common. Therefore, in the workplace, these skills hold more value. They can make or break a team, a brand, a culture, and a company. These include interpersonal skills, communication skills, or any skill that is more liquid in nature. Such as...

✦ Teamwork, Collaboration, & Interpersonal Relations

- An Ability to Navigate Personality Types
- Conflict Resolution

✦Communication skills (Clear & Thorough Verbal, Non-Verbal, & Written Communication)
  - Empathy
  - Situational Observation
  - Non-Defensive Communication
  - Active Listening
  - Mediation
  - Diplomacy
  - Honesty
  - Transparency
- Emotional Intelligence
  - Feedback
  - Failure
  - Work Ethic
  - Quality of Work
  - Work Style
  - Performance Standard
  - Status Quo Versus Extra Mile
  - Self-Awareness
  - Stress
- Time Management & Organization
  - Fail-safes/Planning for Contingencies
  - Systems & Processes
- Problem-Solving Skills
  - Prioritizing
  - Multitasking
  - Adaptability
  - Calculated Risk
  - Resourcefulness

- ✦ Creativity
- ✦ Leadership Skills
  - ✦ Taking Ownership
  - ✦ Taking Responsibility
  - ✦ Weaknesses & Strengths
  - ✦ Trust Skills (team building - key holder - high cash management - PR - client relations)

In the next chapter, we are going to dive deeper into your soft skills and elaborate on how they can contribute to your professional worth.

EDUCATION

Education is more than just your degree or academic scores. It doesn't matter whether your professional education was formal, self-taught, learned through life lessons, mentorships, or online courses. Education is what you have learned that contributed to developing your hard and soft skills as a professional. It even counts if a professor shared insights or offered advice that altered your worldview.

If you started or belonged to a club, community or organization, and held responsibilities that supported that group, those are leadership skills worth advertising, or at the very least worth not leaving on the table. If you attended talks, seminars, workshops, it all counts. Even the examples our parents set and life lessons or advice they imparted matter.

This leads to what you did with your education. Have you passed your wisdom and lessons onto others? Did you mentor newcomers or less experienced colleagues?

Did you pass on tips and tricks of your trade? These are coaching skills which showcase leadership potential.

Next, we come to those mistakes, missteps, failures, setbacks, false moves, and life lessons that set you back or knocked you down. Many hesitate to share these out of a fear of judgment. Those who do are more likely to repeat their mistakes rather than learn from them.

> *No one can hold over you*
> *that which you already own.*

A professional never hides their mistakes. CEOs agree that failure is essential for success. Taking ownership reflects confidence and growth. These are the traits of someone who is constantly evolving and learning.

Granted, if you made a mistake that cost your company revenue or assets, show some discretion with which details you volunteer. You don't have to lie about it. Just be filtered. Present yourself as an asset rather than a liability. This showcases experience, emotional maturity, and adaptability.

CHARITABLE WORK

Detail any volunteering you've done, any charity work, causes you advocate for, or issues where you've served as an activist, and any issue or causes which you support. Even though this might not end up on your customized cover letter or resume, it is important information to collect on yourself. Such topics often come up in interviews. These also serve to help you align a potential employer's moral compass with your own.

Additionally, showcasing your community involvement is beneficial for PR and implies that you would be an excellent representative for their organization. A person who goes beyond expectations, embraces work, and embodies loyalty and dedication stands to serve the interests of most organizations.

CARTOGRAPHING YOUR CAREER PLAN

Once you've answered most of these questions about yourself, and have a pretty thorough curriculum vitae, organize it and map out your career journey, and from there, refine your career plan. This is going to serve as a template for every responsibility you are interested in taking on, and every promotion you are vying for. What are your attainable short-term and long-term goals? Map out each milestone you need to reach to get from point A to point B.

Let's say you're a public relations manager and dream of one day being a partner. Making that leap from where you are standing may seem impossible. But, by breaking every goal up into several smaller, more attainable goals, you're setting realistic expectations and timelines. Dividing each goal into smaller goals, from next week, month, quarter, year, or five years, can make those goals attainable. Especially when you are constantly updating your career plan, determining exactly where you are, and how far you need to go to get to your destination. Doing this will also help you customize and align your career plan to any company.

If, after examining your career history, you realize your career has stalled, that's fine. What counts are the life lessons you learned along the way. The greater your emotional intelligence and growth, the greater your professional worth. This is a fact. Next, it's time to create a timeline for your professional journey.

You cannot map out where you are going without first tracing back how far you've come.

Let's say you had a childhood dream of creating an app-driven dog walking business. Did you know this from the start, or did you only know that you wanted to work with technology and animals, and figured everything else out as you went along? Trace back the complete picture of your career journey. Examine your education, and how that influenced your career. How did each company or organization you worked for further your goals?

Collectively, these will help you come up with even more actionable tangibles, which increase your professional worth. This will help you determine how far and quickly you've advanced your career, and better gauge whether your career has progressed at your desired rate. Once you have all of that information, you'll be better positioned to construct a fresh timeline, and how quickly you can accelerate your career from here.

YOUR PROFESSIONAL BIOGRAPHY

We've now addressed key questions about your professional self and ideal company—as outlined in your updated career plan. What comes next is your story. We must create a comprehensive narrative about your professional identity. Career journeys aren't always linear, and they don't have to be.

Once you've composed your professional biography, we're going to set that aside and write a shorter one. The longer and shorter versions both hold value. Once you have both, it's time to write an even shorter one, and you're going to repeat this process until you have your *kitchen sink biography*. A *kitchen sink biography* is the template for your elevator pitch. It's the core message of who you are as a professional. It's your brand. It's the way you get a following. Whether you are trying to land an interview, whether you are networking, or whatever your goal, you want several bios which all will serve different purposes.

Your longer bio can go in a blog on your website or on your professional social media. When you have more to say than what would fit on your cover letter or resume, make it easy for recruiters to find that extra info when they stalk you online. It's their job, after all, to learn everything they can about you to help determine whether you are the right fit for pursuing a professional relationship with.

YOUR COVER LETTER & RESUME

After compiling your CV, Career Plan, and Biographies, you can take all of that information and compose the templates for your cover letter and resume. Now that you have plenty of material, structure your resume accordingly. Your comprehensive CV allows you to customize and align what you offer as a professional with the opportunity you are vying for. So for now, create a bullet-pointed timeline of your career journey, from education to volunteer experience, to jobs you've held, and anything that applies. As for what skills and traits you list, you can customize those later depending on who you are submitting your resume to.

Remember, these are templates, because every cover letter, resume, and career plan will need to be customized to any specific career opportunity. Let's assume you're pursuing a new job. One of the first steps to customizing your resume is changing its formatting and font to resemble the font and layouts of the pages on their website.

For example, imagine you are applying for a job at Trader Joe's, a household name of a grocery store. Did you know they have their own font, made by and for their company? Now, imagine you download their font and use it for your resume. The signal that sends them shows you already feel you are one of them and are ready to represent their brand. Right away, this will impress, stand out, and potentially earn their trust.

Customize your resume and cover letter to align your brand and story with theirs. Recruiters vigilantly look out for imposters and candidates who pretend to be the ideal hire. So, sincerity counts. If you refer to yourself as incurably honest, and one of the company's core values is integrity, the message is the same, and you can easily adapt your language to theirs or at least meet them halfway to convey that you are genuine and not just a copycat.

In order to convey who you are as a professional, you'll need to be adept at conveying who you are as a person. You see, the skills you build professionally more often than not contribute to enhancing your personal life and thereby impact who you are as a human being. Therefore, the two are interconnected.

Next chapter, we'll explore contextualizing your identity in relatable terms. We'll also touch on how to actionably showcase all your soft skills in real time. The more we measurably define who you are as a professional, the greater your perceived worth. And every single detail incrementally increases your value.

Chapter 2
Who Are You?

L ast chapter, we covered everything you have to offer, according to your own perspective and the perspective of others. We discussed documenting what you are celebrated for and creating a database of everything you have to offer as a professional.

This comprehensive CV database needs to be constantly updated. It is the foundation for your professional worth, enabling you to adapt it to any company, position, or purpose. As you uncover more skills, more talents and gifts, more character traits and expertise, you'll just continue to add to, and fine-tune, your CV.

From your setbacks to your accomplishments, to your drive and ambition, you'll continue mapping out not only where you've been, but where you are going. This documents all the bare facts and statistics of who you are as a professional, including your experience and skills, and the twists and turns of your career journey, stripped of emotional content.

Chapter one focused on collecting your professional data. This next chapter focuses on defining your professional and personal identity and presenting your career journey in the perfect light. After all, the attitude you present it with will alter the context of your narrative. We'll also explore what kind of work you prefer, what you are good at, and why. If you went to college or university, it is highly likely that your instructors taught you about the concepts of soft skills, such as time management. We'll explore this as well. Even when instructed on such concepts, putting them into practice is a different ordeal. Like gauging distance, measuring the time it takes to accomplish several tasks can prove challenging.

While exploring this, we are going to refine your systems approach for demonstrating these skills in *actionable terms,* even when discussing them. Saying you're great at time management only says it and proves nothing. Whereas explaining the steps you take to ensure you plan for everything systematically, actionably shows your thinking through your choice of words. Mastering this will increase your professional worth and heighten your perceived skill level, showcasing that you are who you claim to be.

So, let's dive into how contextualizing your soft skills will increase your worth, such as taking ownership of your narrative, being in complete control of your attitude, worldview, and showcasing your actionable determination.

THE JOB OF THE RECRUITER

Always remember, the better you understand a recruiter's job and their goals, the better you'll understand your audience. Think of a recruiter as a team builder. They're seeking a strong candidate who aligns well with their culture and colleagues. Whereas you're interested in learning more about the position you are interviewing for to make sure it is the ideal job for you. You both, interviewer and interviewee, want something. So, we'll also cover how you can simplify your path to success by aligning your objectives with theirs.

We'll cover this more deeply in section two, but it is important to understand that it's a recruiter's job to build upon and nurture their teams. Each person's contribution shapes the work culture, including their attitude and morale. Your worldview and mindset influence how others perceive you, what they value you for, which thereby impacts your perceived value.

How you go about building relationships with those you work with correlates with how effectively you can earn their trust. Those who are singularly focused on advancing their own goals are less likely to be trusted than those who aim to further the goals of the team.

Consistency equals reliability. The more reliable you are, the more your fellow teammates and leaders will turn to you for knowledge, advice, mentoring, and coaching.

PERSONALITY & BEHAVIORAL FACTORS

There are various approaches to commanding your professional worth. Some are more passive, while others are more assertive, and this depends on whether you have a more introverted or extroverted personality. If you are more introverted, don't assume taking an assertive approach is better. One must always act according to their own nature.

This leads to our next exercise: *Know Thyself!* Now that you've compiled your CV database, you'll be better prepared to interview yourself. The aim of your self-interview is to assess your experience level and skills, while practicing how to communicate them. This will also help clarify how far you have to go to get to where you are going, and how quickly it will take you to get there. With a clearer map, you will exponentially increase your worth.

Start by determining if you are an introvert, extrovert, or ambivert. Why is this important? It can help you fine-tune what the perfect job, environment, and career look like to you. This will inform you, and the recruiter, of how happy you would be in a role, and thereby how sustainable an employee you would be. It assists recruiters and companies in evaluating your fit for the job, and potentially matching you with a more suitable position. Understanding where you fall on the scale now, as opposed to when the question is cleverly posed in an interview, will also equip you to deliver more confident answers.

But, regardless of where you fall on the scale, you'll want to showcase that you're effective at building relationships. This is more important than anything, especially when it is the recruiter's job to find the perfect candidate to complement their current teams. Therefore, how well one works and plays with others will impact their decision of whom they'll hire. Lastly, this will simplify the job of the recruiter, or the algorithmic interview assessment model, when profiling your behavior.

Knowing this about yourself, and confidently advertising it at the right time, positions you as a top performer. Your job satisfaction directly impacts your sustainability as an employee. The more you enjoy your work, the more of a thriving career you'll have. Finding a job or career that accommodates your personality and enables you to do the work you are good at makes the difference between one's job satisfaction and burning out. It's a straightforward way for interviewers to assess success. So, it's integral that you be honest with yourself here. Only the dishonest answer is incorrect. Remember, when you don't act according to your own nature, it will come across as disingenuous, and it will cause you to trip yourself up.

So, when interviewing yourself, start by asking why you have chosen the profession you are in. Did you fall into your career or did you pursue it? Are you chasing the money, or are you passionate about your work? Are you happy? To better answer that, examine what work environment allows you to maximize your productivity while enhancing your work-life balance. Doing this will help you better understand how to define your brand, professional purpose statement, your mission statement, your core values, your pillars, and how representative they are of the career path you are on, which we'll cover more in the next chapter.

YOUR BEHAVIORAL MODEL

Introvert versus extrovert—it is rare that someone falls under one extreme or another. Understanding whether you imagine yourself as more of an extrovert who thrives on collaborating and engaging with others, or an introvert who prefers more solitary tasks and activities, will help inform your narrative and messaging. An ambivert is usually seen as the most desirable. They are more adaptable, reliable, ambidextrous, and varied in their talents.

An extrovert excels as a team player, collaborating cross-functionally with other departments and delivering exceptional customer service. Extroverts thrive on, and are recharged through, group activities and collaborating with others. Yet, although they traditionally build stronger relationships, they often socialize more, and are less productive than some of their introverted counterparts.

Introverts typically have a stronger attention to detail and thrive on performing repetitive and monotonous tasks of a more singularly focussed analytical nature. Such as compiling reports, research, or programming, to name a few. They are also traditionally reliable *go-to resources for information.* They tend to focus more on key performance indicators and data than on boosting morale and building relationships. They need to be alone to recharge and prefer to keep their head down rather than touting their own laurels.

Ambiverts are not perfectly in the middle but closer to the center on either side of the scale. An ambivert's rechargeable environment determines their position on that scale. For example, an ambivert who enjoys working in collaborative team environments, but needs alone time to recharge their battery, would lean more on the introverted side of that scale. Whereas a pragmatic individual who has a strong attention to detail and uncanny focus, who may need to recharge by interacting with others, would be more of an extrovert.

I am closer to being an ambivert than a pure introvert. I can be very extroverted in my comfort zone, like with familiar teammates or at a party with people I know. However, in situations where I'm surrounded by unfamiliar faces, like parties where I only know the person who invited me or whom I'm accompanying, I become extremely shy and hesitant to engage. Also, when in consecutive social situations, my battery runs low and the only way I can recharge is when I am alone.

CULTURAL INDIVIDUALITY & CONFORMITY

Remember, not every company that claims they are an equal opportunity employer is telling the truth. Experience is everything. If a company doesn't have real-world experience in cultural competence, then their DEI statements will have little backing to them. So, how do you identify whether a company is culturally competent and truly embraces equality and inclusion in the workplace? Start by questioning how bold they are. Do they conform or do they embrace individuality?

It takes courage to explore, and to show interest in the experiences of others who come from different backgrounds than your own, to celebrate differences and to advertise this with pride. It takes courage to step outside of your comfort zone and to challenge others to do the same.

Without courageous curiosity, compassion, or a willingness to explore, one can never truly compare their own struggles or opportunities to someone else's. So, this is how you should determine how open, varied, and unique their work culture is. When you look at their teams, is everyone uniform in their representation of the company, or is it representative of diverse and equitable individuality?

'The reward for conformity is that everyone likes you but yourself.' - Rita Mae Brown

You need to hold yourself accountable to your worth. You need to maintain who you are, your individuality, and your dignity. The taller and prouder you stand with your chin up, the greater the perception of your worth. Lastly, if an employer advertises everyone has a voice in their work culture, how have they genuinely put that to the test? And, if everyone does have a voice, do you know what you want to say? If not, how do you expect to be heard?

You see, disagreement is essential to innovation, and doesn't have to translate to conflict. An emotionally intelligent individual finds the middle ground, successfully navigates personality clashes rather than seeing their differences as an obstacle. They are not afraid of being challenged or challenging others. They are constructive and team-oriented. And, they make their voice heard, because they care.

STRUCTURAL INTEGRITY

The structure of your character is informed by your moral compass, your ethics, your style, and integrity. I like the use of the word integrity here. *Structural integrity* directly refers to how adequately something supports the weight of itself. So this is how I view integrity when it pertains to one's character.

The core of character distills down to your structural integrity. That which holds you together. And someone with great professional worth is strong and can hold up even under the greatest stress. If someone isn't true to their word, or true to themself, they have a low moral compass and lack integrity. In turn, they are weak of character. For example, someone who would try to hide their mistakes or missteps, or who would take the credit for another's accomplishments, or compromise their employer's assets, is a liability. They would hurt the bottom line, damage morale, could potentially burn out other members of the team, and sow dissent. This is someone who has little professional worth.

Now consider the strength of the team as a whole— how well everyone gets along, and how effectively they all collaborate. If the structural integrity of one teammate's character cannot even support their own weight, how can they support the weight of the rest of the team? Whereas someone who sees a chance to develop the team, advancing their goals, and takes pride in their part as a stakeholder in the team's success is an asset who builds trust, creates opportunity, boosts morale, and makes the team stronger as a whole. They all need to be unified and support each other with strength.

All of this boils down to character. Therefore, the strength of your character will directly impact whether you earn and retain the trust of others, determining the strength of the relationships you build, your brand of teamwork, collaboration, your capacity for innovation, and your career. Consider this when conveying your professional worth.

WRITTEN, VERBAL, & NON-VERBAL COMMUNICATION

Communication skills are crucial, and don't simply refer to how eloquently spoken you are, or how extensive your vocabulary is. In fact, people will more often communicate nonverbally than verbally. So, always be self-aware of how you present yourself. Strong communication means having patience, empathy, and being able to communicate non-defensively, which is nuanced. This requires diplomacy, being a mediator, possessing situational observation skills, active listening, and being able to mirror what others are communicating to you while validating their concerns.

It requires honesty, transparency, and displaying cultural competence pertaining to socio-economic status, gender, identity, race, religion, and geographical factors. And, one of the most important things to remember here is that you will be evaluated for your communication skills throughout your professional career, starting with your interview. How one communicates daily will inform an employer of your attitude through the words you choose, and whether they can trust you to represent their brand and serve as the voice for their organization.

It also pertains to how effectively you adapt your communication style to others. The stronger communicator must go the distance in any situation. Rarely does one meet the other person halfway. Make your expertise actionable by communicating complex topics in simple terms. Or, if someone is communicating and responding emotionally to a situation, and you are more emotionally intelligent in that moment than the person you're discoursing with, it's incumbent on you to maintain the higher ground, and patiently communicate non-defensively until that higher ground becomes common ground.

Possessing strong communication skills is also core to navigating the unavoidable politics in every work environment every day. We'll touch on this more later on, and how your communication skills impact your professional worth.

EMOTIONAL INTELLIGENCE

There is a common human phenomenon I cannot thoroughly explain. You see, more often than not, people will almost always tell you who they are right off the bat. Perhaps everyone yearns for acceptance, and needs to tell you, point blank, both the good and bad about themselves. For example, on our first date, my wife told me she is complicated, and therefore leads a complicated life. Whereas I am pretty basic, and at that time led a pretty simple life. We've been married a long time now, and my life has grown to be pretty darn complicated, through osmosis. But, in all fairness, she did warn me.

I can't even count the number of times I had just met someone, and once they felt comfortable, they shared some unflattering anecdote, such as telling me how they have a hot temper, can say really cruel and hurtful things, and that they sometimes become unhinged. Now, most people mistakenly assume, when someone confides such information, that somehow they will be an exception. But in truth, that is rarely the case. Don't be surprised when that person loses their temper and says something cruel and hurtful to you. It was a warning, shared without boundaries, out of a desperate need to be accepted, without holding themself accountable for it. Maybe they feel exempt from being held accountable since it was served as a disclaimer?

This is something you, as a professional, must constantly be aware of. Practice being reserved and transparent. Honest, yet boundaried. Also, carefully listen to what every potential employer tells you about themselves. Always watch out for red flags and be careful who you choose to work for. I have turned down jobs in the past based on this alone. Anyone who interviews you is a representative of that organization. What they voluntarily reveal may essentially inform you what working with them for the long term will really be like.

For example, I once interviewed for a management position and had a positive rapport with the owner. In fact, he offered me that job and more money than he could afford to pay. But I turned it down, because in the last stages of the interviewing process he told me his staff loves him as much as they hate him, and he told me point blank I would hate him more than I loved him, but that I would love him too as a boss. I appreciated that red flag. I didn't want to work for someone who offered me an assurance that I'd hate him. Even though he disguised it as an off-handed remark, he was telling me the truth.

Another facet of emotional intelligence is one's motivation to develop and grow. How quickly you grow is directly connected to how swiftly you're able to advance your career goals.

A career-minded professional is eager to grow, to learn, and to overcome every growth opportunity they can identify. They understand that when it comes to performance reviews and feedback, no news is the antithesis of good news. No news means your performance is underwhelming or unseen. So a career-minded professional is someone who is proactively seeking feedback. This is someone who wants to learn how they are perceived by others so they can reclaim their own narrative. They are plugged in to what they are responsible for. They actively listen, take notes, record every accomplishment, and diligently self-evaluate. They don't apologize or take the fall for others. They only take ownership of what they should, while demonstrating growth.

The same goes for their attitude towards failure. Setbacks can be hard to deal with, but must be taken in stride. Someone who quickly dusts off, examines what went wrong, learns from it, and tries again is far more likely to succeed than someone who takes longer to recover, or is increasingly hard on themself. Even worse is that individual who tries to hide their mistakes rather than learn from them. It is then highly probable for such an individual to repeat that mistake again and again.

A HIGH EQ INCREASES YOUR WORTH

It is time to look at yourself under a microscope, and to identify your strengths and your growth opportunities, personally and professionally. Notice I don't use the word weakness here. Context, attitude, and narrative is the name of the game. So, instead of weakness, we'll use the term growth opportunity.

This single shift in contextualizing alters perspective, attitude, and thereby changes outcome.

Be transparent and honest with yourself about your growth opportunities. If you aren't completely honest with yourself, you won't be able to move forward. Moreover, it's just you here. Being honest with yourself shows strength. It shows that you are worthy of the opportunity to grow. So, if you're not accustomed to this, practice.

Admitting to yourself those areas where you need to grow shows you take ownership of your growth opportunities, that you learn from them, and take responsibility for them. Saying it out loud creates a safe space to shape your narrative, and contextualize that weakness as a growth opportunity, which presents you as an asset rather than a liability.

So, examining both your hard and soft skills, admit out loud where you've failed in the past. Discuss those setbacks with yourself. Did you take responsibility? What did you learn from that experience? How do you plan to apply those life lessons to ensure you don't repeat those mistakes? Be free here. Remember, this isn't a formal interview, it's just you.

Imagine there was a time when you disregarded your instincts and followed the misguided advice of someone you trusted. Now imagine that resulted in a failure. Blaming them suggests you've learned nothing from the experience. You decided to take their advice, so the responsibility falls on your shoulders. As a starting point, you need to hold yourself accountable for your decision.

Consider an alternate perspective: you listened to advice, heard it, and found merit in it. These are strengths worth repeating. The growth opportunity was not looking further into their approach, or asking if it was the right approach for *you* to take. That's the situation when scrutinized. And, if you choose to make a similar choice again, you'll go in prepared to take responsibility for that calculated risk.

Admitting to a setback reflects emotional intelligence and suggests you've grown from the experience and are less likely to repeat it. Admitting you made mistakes and have grown from them displays strength and confidence in your abilities.

You cannot attain success without first experiencing humble growth from failure.

LEADERSHIP SKILLS

A leader is someone who takes charge of their own development, takes ownership of their role, is a stakeholder, and is self-aware of the growth opportunities and strengths of not only themself, but the other members of their team.

Ultimately, when you take charge of your own career and take actionable steps towards getting what you want, you are leading. Leading by example means supporting the goals of the team, embracing the objectives of your organization as your own, setting the pace and the attitude, all while boosting morale. Your attitude dictates your behavior and informs your decision-making. You're unafraid to respectfully challenge authority. You mentor others, share your knowledge, manage up, actively listen, learn, and anticipate need. You're a relationship builder, can communicate vision, and understand the value of delegating or requesting help when needed.

A leader understands that the only way to innovate is to learn first. You have to know the rules before you break them, and you have to know why they invented the wheel and the purpose it serves before even entertaining reinventing that wheel. A leader understands that trust must be earned and relationships built through the integrity of one's character.

PROBLEM-SOLVING SKILLS

Solving problems requires scaling priorities, being able to multitask, and being able to adapt and respond situationally rather than emotionally in fast-paced, high-stressed situations. It displays whether you can think quickly on your feet or if you allow your stress to dictate your responses through task paralysis or task procrastination. I look at problem-solving skills as common sense. This pertains to whether you work smarter versus working harder.

Problem-solving is also about your approach to thinking outside of the box. It reveals how resourceful you are when you don't have the information needed to make an informed decision. It dictates how you approach taking risks. Someone who is a risk-taker is not necessarily an asset, nor is someone who is risk-averse. Rather, someone who gathers information quickly and takes an informed and educated calculated risk is more likely thinking in the best interest of all other stakeholders and would be viewed as an asset.

The biggest benefit of preparing how to communicate your approach to solving problems is being able to deliver your message with consistency and confidence. It showcases that you have a strong work ethic and know your job backwards and forwards. How you define your approach to solving problems will help you also convey, in actionable terms, your approach and whether you can walk the walk and talk the talk.

TIME MANAGEMENT & ORGANIZATION

Time management ties directly into your problem-solving abilities. The truest measure of someone who solves problems is someone who plans for those problems before they are even aware of them. It suggests your full view of the big picture. For example, if you set deadlines that allow room for error, planning for the likely event of some unforeseen contingency, you likely have strong time management skills and often deliver ahead of your deadline. This directly connects to a person's work-life balance as well.

Imagine someone, on a Tuesday morning, who hits their snooze button numerous times. When they finally get up, they hurriedly shower, watching the clock tick as they become increasingly aware they are going to be late. They get in their car and realize their gas tank is near empty, and didn't plan on poor traffic on their route.

When they arrive at work they're stressed, and this impacts their attitude, which negatively infects workplace morale and impacts their performance. When their shift is done, they carry the stress of that workday home with them, reducing their quality of life. They neglect to address the mundane responsibilities while they try to recover emotionally, which contributes to a poor night's sleep, which feeds into hitting the snooze button too many times the next day, and it all repeats.

Now, someone who fills up their gas tank on the way home from work, sets out their work clothes the night before, prepares their lunch in advance, and pays attention to traffic conditions before they get in the car has strong time management skills. Someone who is an expert at time management might even schedule unscheduled time in their week, where they prepare for their personal and professional week in advance. Whether that includes preparing meals for the week, doing all laundry on that day, making sure their life is orderly, organized, and every possible predictable contingency is expected and planned for, leaves room for those unforeseen contingencies.

This way, when things don't go according to plan, their stress is less likely to impact their decision making, and they can showcase greater emotional intelligence and a strong work ethic.

This approach to time management also showcases your problem-solving skills, how organized you are, and your approach to your SOPs (systems and processes).

PERFORMANCE STANDARD

How hard you work is a predictor of how often you go the extra mile. A work standard that aims to best your personal best suggests that when you go above and beyond, it goes further than just one extra mile.

Whereas a work standard that typically falls within the usual distance traveled–that of simply meeting expectations–reflects someone who hits cruise control and has a minimal work ethic. It also suggests a lack of self-awareness and a disinterest in advancing the goals of their team.

How would you score yourself on all the topics we've discussed so far?

1) Room for Growth
2) Signs of Growth
3) Meets Expectations
4) Occasionally Exceeds Expectations
5) Consistently Goes Above & Beyond

What comments would you insert under your score? What advice would you give yourself? And what opportunities for growth can you identify?

Constantly conducting self-evaluations on every aspect of who you are as a professional will help determine where you stand in your career progression. Even when you have room to grow and are driven to best your personal best, also focus on where you shine, such as your drive for professional growth.

Chapter 3
Where Do You Come From &
Where Are You Going?

WHERE ARE YOU?

Let's take a closer look at where you're at in your career. You cannot mistake your current location for your desired destination, which lies further up the road. Orient yourself by focusing on the road ahead. How far away does that feel? What milestones do you need to pass to get there?

WHY ARE YOU HERE?

How did you get here? Was it by accident or through intention? Do you feel your career has stalled? If so, why? How focussed are your intentions right now? Are your motives pure and are you making your decisions for all the right reasons? Are there multiple truths to that answer? How would you define your reality?

WHERE ARE YOU GOING?

Early on, I had a colleague who suggested I needed to learn how to be selfish if I wanted to rise up in my career and actually attain what I was after. I took his advice to heart. I advise you to do the same.

What do you want? Is this the right direction for you? Have you always been heading here, or should you change course? Is the door you're about to knock on the correct one? Is this the correct time, place, or door to knock on?

With some digging, it won't be hard to guess what's behind door #1, #2, or #3. By choosing the right door, you might propel yourself further along your path. Choose the wrong door, and you may find yourself leagues behind where you stand. Most importantly, whatever decision you make should only be made on your own behalf, rather than trying to please someone else. This includes your parents, your significant other, or your superiors. Ensure the path you choose is the right path for you.

If your workplace has a shortage of supervisors and has pressured you into a leadership position that is counter-intuitive to your goals, carefully consider whether the skills you'd gain from that detour would come at a greater benefit or greater cost to the big picture of your career.

Let's say your parents run a convenience store and dream of passing the store down to you one day. Was that your dream, or to become an engineer and escape the family business? If you're unsure of what you want, then what you want may not have yet presented itself. So, try not to settle. Keep looking. And remember, luck is where you find it, and you have to look for it. So, keep the path clear for the perfect opportunity to present itself.

WHERE DO YOU COME FROM?

Before you can successfully reach your destination, you need to first be able to articulate where you've come from. You've already mapped out your career journey. However, you need to be able to speak about the companies or organizations you previously worked with. For example, imagine you are in an interview, and are asked:

I see you worked at *Dingus Widget International Incorporated*. Tell me about that company.

How you answer that question can increase or decrease the perception of your professional worth.

You see, every company, organization, non-profit, and foundation has a brand and culture. This is typically composed of a purpose statement, a mission statement, core values, pillars, and a work environment designed to foster innovation. Throughout all of these, they'll have their own branding language as well. Their representatives–trustworthy employees whose values align with theirs–must embody this language and conduct both on and off the clock.

So, when a recruiter asks about your previous employers, the manner in which you answer will inform them of how effectively you served as a representative, and whether you could be trusted to represent their brand as well. Your answer will also inform them of whether you felt aligned with the values and priorities of your previous employers, or whether they were just take-it-or-leave-it jobs.

But that's not the whole big picture. The better you understand all of your prior employers–how they are similar and how they stand apart–will help you clarify the narrative of your career path. Were you pressured into a leadership role that derailed your career? Were their promises for career advancement not as advertised? Were their company values aligned with your own, and did they stand behind and embody their own values?

Lastly, beyond fine-tuning *your* narrative, you need to define *your* purpose statement, *your* mission statement, *your* core values, *your* pillars, and *your* ideal work environment for facilitating innovation. It starts with revisiting your career map. Then, you need to go to the website of every previous employer. What do they all have in common? How do they relate to the companies you dream of working for? Do they align with your priorities? What was their code of ethics and did they stick to them? Did they embody their values? And what leadership style do they promote?

UNDERSTANDING A COMPANY'S CULTURE

When a candidate shows an understanding of a company's values, mission, purpose, environment, and pillars, and adopts their culture-language into their own, it showcases a strong work ethic, strong communication skills, and motivation for wanting to work for them. Better understanding these principles will help you align yourself with the perfect employer, ensuring you are not only happy where you work, but that you'll land somewhere that you'll feel celebrated for your merits and valued for what you offer.

This also makes a recruiter feel validated, heard, related to, empathized with, and helps earn their trust while offering you more credibility as a candidate.

Here is a brief explanation of every building block of a company's culture. And, as each is explained, ask yourself what *your* purpose statement is, *your* mission statement, values, and so on.

A PURPOSE STATEMENT

A company's purpose statement describes why they are passionate about doing what they do. It's what gives them, or the business, meaning. It's what motivates them and suggests their value to their audience/ potential clients, and the impact they aim to have on who they are serving. Companies use purpose statements to help drive their mission and goals forward.

A MISSION STATEMENT

When understanding a company's Mission Statement, think of it like a military operation. They are assembling hand-picked teams to execute their mission. It is their calling, and it's the big picture they ultimately aim to achieve. This includes their overall objectives. A company's mission statement supports their vision, serves to communicate their purpose, their commitment, and direction. A mission statement explains their reason for existence, for doing what they do.

It is their end goal... Mission success.

CORE VALUES

A company's core values are their guiding principles. These support their vision, shape their culture, and light the way for their teams and stakeholders. They inform and remind them of their identity, of who they are, in principle and in character. They align every single business decision they make with these values. Many companies are quoted as saying, *"A business without core values isn't really a business."* Or, *"A business without values is a business at risk."* You see, teams unaware of their identity cannot effectively represent or embrace the brand's culture.

PILLARS

A company's pillars are the heart of their code of conduct. This is their sense of ethics; integrity, transparency, always doing the right thing, etcetera. Members of their organization are expected to follow this conduct model, both during and outside of work hours. It guides them towards their success through a shared passion for their purpose, while living by their core values. Their pillars are responsible for upholding the structural integrity of their organization's character.

WORK ENVIRONMENT

A company's environment is integral to the team culture which they aim to build and support. This is the model for their unique working environment and how they attract and retain their target talent. It's what makes their employee structure function optimally. Flex work schedule, self-managed employees, departmental communications, and positioning each employee or recruit to work in their ideal environment are all components of ensuring they are supporting their people to perform at their best.

HOW TO APPLY THEM TO YOURSELF

What would your purpose statement, mission statement, core values, pillars, and a well-defined work environment look like? My purpose statement, for instance, could be to increase your net worth, while helping you fulfill your dreams.

My mission statement could be to coach others with passion, help them to rise up, make their dreams come true, and clear a path through the weeds towards the road to success. My core values are Integrity, Communication, Know The Rules Before You Break Them, Write Ethically and With Passion, and Writing Should Be Fun.

My pillars are centered on being honest, transparent, and being responsible for my own actions. It is crucial to ensure a good fit for a working relationship. As for my work environment, it needs to be peaceful, free of distractions, full of natural light, with the sounds of nature or motivating instrumental music.

These will help define your professional identity. Look within, be honest about the decisions that brought you here. Even that which drove you to reading this book. Once you possess this final piece of your puzzle, you'll be in a better position to identify the next appropriate career move for you. Most importantly, it will help you rise up and stand out from the competition in the talent pool.

HOW TO IDENTIFY THE RIGHT OPPORTUNITY WITH THE RIGHT COMPANY AT THE RIGHT TIME

With a clearer sense of your offerings and career goals, you can map out your next career stages and how to reach them. While job hunting, prioritize company fit over mere skill alignment. To identify the right fit, you have to do your research and due diligence. Extensively research every company you are interested in working for. Read up on their branding, purpose, mission, values, principles, pillars, environment, and culture.

In most cases, you will know rather quickly, based on a company's image and reputation, whether theirs is the right environment for you. Read employee reviews, see what media coverage they have, and whether there are any union issues or legal issues they've been facing. But, once you've gotten past these issues, you'll have to judge exactly how far they can take your career.

DIVERSITY, EQUALITY, & INCLUSION

Not long ago, a person of color submitted their resume multiple times for a job. After repeated rejections, they wondered if the recruiter had identified their name as that belonging to a person of color. So, they changed the name on the same resume to a name more commonly applied to a white male. Immediately, they were called and invited for an interview. The applicant refused the interview and sued for discrimination instead. A brave move to incite change.

"Sexism and racism are parallel problems. You can compare them in some ways, but they're not at all the same. But they're both symptoms inside the white male power structure."

- Frida Kahlo

Despite numerous companies laying claim to being an equal opportunity employer, their truth lies with whom they employ, which reflects their brand of progress and innovation.

So, read up on the company's DEI statement, accomplishments, and try to determine if they've had any negative media coverage. Also, check out their employee reviews. Then visit their DEI statement page and decide for yourself how sincere they seem. For most companies, it is nothing more than webpage wallpaper. Not to mention, those images of diverse people happily working together are most likely stock images and not representative of their workforce.

But, at a quick glance, you can take a look at their leadership page on their website. How well does their executive team reflect diversity, equality, and inclusion? If their leadership teams, whether their board of directors, executives, or management, represent sincere DEI, that could be a good indication they are indeed an equal opportunity employer.

PRACTICE TAKEN IN STRIDE

You should be ready for the right job when it presents itself, as opposed to being ready for any random job right now. Plan ahead and be prepared at a moment's notice. You want to customize all of your materials to that opportunity. The recruiter will notice, and it conveys a strong work ethic, a keen attention to detail, and advanced communication skills. It also implies your hunger for this opportunity and your inclination towards a long-term fit for the right reasons. The recruiter will view you as a safe investment, which exponentially increases your perceived value.

It showcases that you have drive and focus, and are not taking your next career move lightly. It also suggests you've identified an opportunity for growth, and that the direction they can take your career appeals to you. You identify with their brand, culture, and identity, and are attracted to the working environment they offer.

Some may ask; *"Why put in all that effort if they're not going to hire me?*

Putting in that effort helps determine whether they are the type of company that's more likely to hire you than not. Also, if the company does actually seem to demonstrate that they offer equal pay and equal opportunity, and offer pay transparency, then it is worth putting in the work which your job-seeking competitors might not. Being willing to go the distance and put in this kind of work requires the right mindset.

If it's absolutely the right fit for you, you have to be selfish and take what you want. Leverage every advantage and strategic approach to win that interview, and then to win that job. And, when you shift your thinking to a selfish mindset, you'll imagine that job as already yours, and you have to not only want it, but to take it.

When you adopt this mindset, you play the game better than anyone you know. This is the point of this book. The better you play the game, the greater your professional worth. And using the methods in this book will help you to rise up. You are aggressively pursuing your goals, while passively competing at the same time. When your worth is documented and speaks for itself, it removes debate from the equation.

But, let's say you put in the work and didn't land the job. Was it a waste of time? The short answer is no. The long answer is you're forming habits, learning how to improve upon these techniques, while embodying the experienced professional you aim to be, who is in a league of your own.

Once you put in the work, and become a pro at embodying the strongest candidate any company would be fortunate to compete for, then you've exponentially increased your professional worth. After reaching that point, it is truly a numbers game where you'll end up landing that dream job in no time.

This requires improving your skills and your game, using every strategy at your disposal, and being honest through embodying your genuine self. If you are vying for a job that requires far more experience than you now possess, you won't land that job. But if you identify a job that is at your skill level, but doubt your qualifications, that job can still be yours if you prepare and stand behind yourself as your strongest advocate. To get there, research, substantiate, and embody your newly realized professional worth. Believe it and prove it.

You have to know what you're worth before you can expect anyone else to.

HOW TO ALIGN YOURSELF WITH A POTENTIAL EMPLOYER

It's now time to customize your brand to your potential employer. Once you examine and research everything about them–every webpage, every blog, every bit of media and information–examine how they describe their people. Anytime their website describes the qualities that their people/teams/employees embody, they are describing the type of person they are looking to recruit. This is their target talent. This marketing is designed to attract their ideal candidates.

Next, go through all of your materials and do similar research on yourself. Identify every alignment and the pros and cons of working together. This will better equip you for deciding whether pursuing an opportunity with them is the right move, and whether it's worthwhile to customize all your template materials to them.

You're not an imposter. You're simply identifying every similarity and alignment between yourself and their ideal candidate. You are outlining how compatible you are and how well you fit their mold.

TALENT ACQUISITION PLATFORMS & CLOUD BASED RECRUITING SOFTWARE

Most companies use recruiting software, talent acquisition platforms, or HR administration software as tools. These, on the most basic level:

✦ Save time, which translates to saving payroll dollars

✦ Make it easier to track their recruiting marketing efforts–website wallpaper, job posts, hiring platforms, and job boards

✦ Screen applicants' resumes and cover letters

✦ Track where each candidate is in the interview process

✦ Track employee performance, work history, performance reviews, write-ups, salary history, and more

The companies that design such software and platforms are only interested in making money. That's their bottom line. Now, many of them claim they mitigate bias. However, most of them have design flaws. The patches for these flaws are designed with their bottom line in mind. If their algorithm detects a symbol it doesn't recognize, or formatting that it confuses for something else, it will screen out your materials.

Why? Rather than risk their company's reputation (the recruiting platform software company) by forwarding on a resume that they failed to assess to their client (the company you are applying to), they would rather screen you out. What does that represent? A bias towards their interests as opposed to the interests of you or that potential employer.

So, when formatting your resume, avoid using any unique symbols, borders, graphic designs, or photo images. Keep your resume as simple as possible. Additionally, anytime it is an option, you should always apply to the job through the company's website rather than through the job board. Your materials will go through less algorithmic screening, and you'll have a better chance of it getting in front of the right person.

The recruiter's job is to find their ideal candidate as quickly as possible. The sooner that position is filled, and the less time it takes, the less payroll hours spent. The less spent on those job boards, the less exhausted their budget will be. And, the bigger their budget, the more they can afford to pay.

Having said all that, one thing you are going to do is customize the aesthetic of your materials to each potential employer.

CUSTOMIZE YOUR RESUME

Let's now revisit your CV. Examine all the skills and qualities they say they are looking for. Then select all of those from your CV that seem like they would prove of value to that potential employer, and customize your resume accordingly. Keep your resume brief, one to two pages, or as long as the industry standard for your position allows. Stick to your KPIs. Your professional narrative will almost always be viewed as a predictor of future job performance.

When listing each company or organization you've worked for, offer a brief description in one to two sentences describing the company, who they serve and what they offer, and the revenue or goals they've reached. This will save your recruiter the trouble of looking them up while helping them draw parallels between who your employers are and how you are aligned with them.

Next, study their company's website presentation. For example, on their website, look at their company culture statements. How do they use bullet points? What font do they use on their website? There are very simple methods for identifying the font they use. A quick search will guide you through how to look at a website's code and identify their font. There are even easier methods for downloading that font if it is not built into your computer, so that you can customize your materials.

Also, mirror their format on your resume. Do they italicize certain text, like titles and company positions? Where do they use all caps, or underline, or bold print? Not only will this be visually appealing to your audience, it will suggest you go the extra mile in your presentation and research skills just to align yourself with their style guide. Also, mirror their culture language wherever you can. This will suggest you're already effective at representing their brand by adopting it as your own.

When fine-tuning the presentation of your materials, you want to make absolutely sure that the presentation is consistent from beginning to end. So, if your bullet-pointed lists do not have closing punctuation in one sentence, and have closing punctuation in all others, such inconsistencies will suggest your performance standard is likewise inconsistent and unreliable. If the font changes from one section to another, or your previous position titles are italicized for one job, but not the next, this is also inconsistent. It communicates to a recruiter that you do not have a keen attention to detail.

So, make sure everything is uniform. Also, to ensure the language is smooth and easy to read, recite every word you write out loud, or have a language model read it out loud to you. This will help you catch those mistakes which your eyes typically miss.

Lastly, avoid being redundant. Reiterating the same skills over and over under one job will look like you are trying to fluff up your resume. It also suggests you didn't notice you mentioned it before, and don't have a keen eye for the details. If you performed similar job duties from one job to the next, feel free to detail that. This will show your skills are sharp. But, don't repeat information unless it's crucial to your experience or work history.

PERSONALIZE YOUR LETTER

If they advise you to submit your materials through their portal, do that. But, I always recommend padding the job. So, unless it is expressly forbidden, reach out to the company and try to find the name of the hiring authority responsible for interviewing and filling the position you are interested in. When you get the name of the hiring authority, you'll deliver more personalized, and memorable, materials. Getting a direct email address to submit your materials to-in addition to the conventional method-can also help move you to the top of the pile.

Phone calls are better. In person is best. Introduce yourself and state that you wanted to make sure you addressed your customized cover letter to the right person. Try to be personable and go the extra mile. If you end up speaking with that person, ask some pertinent introductory questions about the company and position. Ask if there is anything specific or unique that they are looking for which could give you a competing edge. Thank them for their time and let them know you'll be submitting your materials shortly. Doing this suggests a strong work ethic, that you are interested in building relationships, and that your work standard is above and beyond.

Every person you meet during the application process is an accurate reflection of the company's employees. So, if you have an unpleasant exchange, it might indicate an unpleasant work experience, and it might not be a good fit after all. If in doubt, try to get a more accurate feel for whether it's the right fit.

HOW TO LEARN A COMPANY'S CULTURE OR BRAND LANGUAGE

Again, research their core values, mission, purpose, pillars, etcetera. Read their code of ethical conduct as well, which typically has a letter from their CEO as a forward. Although this is rarely found on a company website, it's often available elsewhere, and easily found with a simple search.

As you research each company, you'll be able to recognize specific keywords and key phrases they repeat throughout their messaging. This is their culture language and is built out by their marketing department. These are typically the adverbs, adjectives, qualifiers, and filler words. Words such as innovative, friendly, passionate, caring, etcetera.

What keywords do they adopt to describe themselves? Do any of those terms apply to you? Make a list of similar professional terms. Try not to copy their language verbatim. Throw some synonyms in with those of theirs which you adopted into your own language. You are going to weave them naturally into your cover letter where you can. It shouldn't be forced either, but organic and according to your own nature. Sincerity is key here.

Attest to why this opportunity is the right career move and the right fit for you, while adapting your language to the company's language. The more you adopt their language as your own, and showcase how you identify, and already embody their culture, the better you'll be at speaking in relatable terms, thereby earning their trust. Communicating in a way that mirrors the character of their company showcases a strong mutual fit, with sincerity, and in accordance with your shared values. This will assure them you could effectively represent their brand while rising up within the company.

WHERE ARE YOU NOW?

Once you know what you want, it is time to adapt. Examine your CV and remind yourself of what your coworkers have said about you, or why they look forward to working with you. Think of work-appropriate examples your family and friends have shared with you over the years. Next, detail how you would define the experience of working with you? Customize your cover letter, resume, career goals, your personal brand of who you are and what you deliver as a professional, and your biographies without repeating in your cover letter what you've already volunteered.

Remember, your cover letter expresses how this organization is aligned and the right fit for you, and what you have to offer them. Whereas your bio is a statement speaking to your professional journey, which has clearly, and with purpose, led you here. Your biography is a brief statement answering those questions:

✦ Who are you?
✦ Where do you come from?
✦ Why are you here, pitching to work for them?
✦ Where are you hoping this professional relationship will lead you next?

You want to communicate everything as clearly as possible. This will showcase your strong communication skills, which increase your worth and make you a more viable candidate. And that's the message you want to send. Every measure you take to showcase your high attention to detail, strong work ethic, and strong communication skills suggests what you have to offer.

In your messaging, by suggesting this feels like the right fit, you can showcase your loyalty potential. By adopting their language, you reveal you are aligned. By stating what attracted you to their company, such as it being a meritocracy with pay transparency, you can communicate it being a company you admire and would be proud to represent for the long term.

When well rehearsed and prepared in advance, you've re-contextualized your narrative, and own it as well. This will enable you to navigate any questions thrown your way with confidence and grace. Let's say an interview question touches on a negative experience in the workplace, such as:

Tell me about a time you experienced a conflict at work?

It is up to you whether you want to share that example, or share a time you experienced a scheduling conflict at work, and how you navigated it. Or, how you walked into a conflict between two other workers, and played mediator.

CONTEXTUALIZE YOUR NARRATIVE

Let's say you worked for a company that you didn't relate to, or whose values didn't align with yours. Or, you worked for a manager that seemed to hold you back, yet promoted your peers. Or, you felt you were unfairly demoted or fired. Whatever the situation, you must never think of yourself as a victim. It is integral that you remain professional at all times. Perception is reality.

If asked why you left your previous job before lining up another and you share negative experiences you had with a supervisor, your recruiter will only see a victim. And a victim is not an asset.

Alternatively, you could explain that the leadership style didn't align with your values or the values of the company. So, rather than working in an environment that was counterintuitive to your own goals while exhausting all your time and energy, you quit. You decided it was more conducive to your goals to dedicate your time to finding a company whose values are more aligned with your own.

Now, that sounds like someone with clear priorities who's carefully planned out their next step, who wants to ensure any next career move is the right move. Even more so, it sounds like the words of a leader who has taken control of their own destiny and showcases integrity by not badmouthing others.

Share what you learned from each job. Portray strength, bridge-building, and professionalism. You are always in control of your own narrative. And that is what this very first step is all about. Maintaining control of your story, of how others perceive you, and giving off an aura of a heightened professional worth. This template defines your identity and attitude, both on and off duty. No one else can control your attitude, and your story is your own.

HOW TO TRANSITION FROM ONE STAGE OF YOUR CAREER TO THE NEXT

First, determine what contributes most to your job satisfaction and what would cause you to feel burned out. And explore what the perfect environmental conditions are for optimizing your productivity and success.

Let's say you are considering leaving a job where you feel marginalized, patronized, and where you feel the leadership is authoritarian. Unsurprisingly, this contributed to a low-performing, demoralized work environment. No one would blame you for wanting to exit that work environment as soon as possible.

But what do you accomplish by quitting your job before lining up another? Doing so exhibits poor planning skills, and will ultimately undermine your confidence, especially when you are running out of money and desperate to find a new job. This will grossly undermine your perceived professional worth.

However, if you are careful in your planning, dedicate enough time to determining which career move is best for you, all while giving more than ample notice to your current employer and going above and beyond to ensure your successor is well-trained and ready to take the mantle, your professional worth is greatly increased. Any recruiter who learns this about a candidate will assume they consistently display integrity and a strong work ethic.

So, with every action you take, you can control your own narrative. Whether you are making a career move to pursue your ideal work environment in a more compatible culture, or are seeking greater opportunity for advancement or an opportunity that can expedite your career progression, it is up to you how you want to contextualize your situation. Perhaps you recognize you are burned out on your job, but the most recent stepping stones of your career have led you to understanding with increased clarity the direction that now feels right to you.

Perhaps you are re-entering the workforce after being self-employed, or after dedicating time to the family business. Maybe your business was a success, and you recently sold it, and it would feel like taking a break working for someone else for a change. Whatever your situation, frame it in a positive growth mindset.

Map out your narrative and shape your reality. Self-evaluate. What have you learned and earned–trust, responsibility, hands-on skills, key holder, high cash handling, everything that wouldn't fit on a resume, every single skill and facet of the work you do? Always look at yourself through the microscope that others might look at you through.

Your attitude informs who you are as a professional. So you always want to take the high road and embody integrity. And build bridges everywhere you can.

IN SUMMARY

Putting in the work to enhance your career and your professional worth takes practicing the right habits, which become easier and more second nature in time.

Decide how you want to be viewed as a professional, and that view will guide your professional journey. Remember, your attitude and the light you see your worldview through informs your narrative. And, if all else fails, be selfish, and think about what you have to gain by doing so. The higher your professional worth, the better your quality of life will be.

Just understand who you are, where you are, and be faithful to yourself. See the value of everything you offer and be true to your own nature. If you read through section one without putting in the work—cataloguing all of your accomplishments, your badges of honor, what feels like the right fit for you, what success looks like, your strengths and weaknesses, your top value propositions and skills, your talents, and gifts, what you are good at, what you love most about your profession, and the work you do—then you haven't yet laid the foundation for your professional worth.

By better understanding your strengths, and the strengths you have yet to acquire, you will fine-tune and define what you are good at, what you enjoy about your work, and all the skills, natural talents, and gifts you possess. Defining all these elements makes you an authority on yourself. Maintaining focus and clarity on what you want, how far you want to go, what you need to learn, and have yet to accomplish, will help you determine whether that job prospect will take you there. When you find the right opportunity, be ready for it, compete for it, and rise up with each experience.

Determine how far you want to go, how you'll get there on your own, and what is standing in your way. If you are your only obstacle, step aside. Silence that voice that says you could never do that, that says you can't accomplish what others have accomplished before you. From now on, we are proving, through a systematic approach, that you are capable of that and more. Don't settle.

Landing a job you might be qualified for, but would be miserable working in, just to generate income, negatively impacts your performance, decreases your professional worth, and your self-worth. Remember, a professional relationship is a committed relationship. And entering into a committed relationship should never be done lightly. Having a clearer idea of your ideal dream job should narrow your search.

In the next section, we are going to further cover what goes into recruiting someone, what a hiring manager or recruiter looks for in every candidate, how difficult their job is, and how you can make their job easier. The motives behind every question they ask in an interview will be explored, along with what they want to hear from each candidate they interview. We will explore every step of the recruiting process, how much it all costs, how it cuts into their budget, and tease apart how much they can afford to pay you.

We'll also dive deep into how to keep your materials fresh and original, from avoiding pitfalls, to negotiating salary, and how there is more to negotiation than just money. For example, you can negotiate for the frequency of your pay increase, whether you'll be eligible for a pay increase in the next cycle, and how to negotiate adhering to the timelines you've detailed in your career plan. This will help you avoid a carrot and stick career progression while continually increasing your perceived value to the organization.

By performing the salary negotiation dance like a true professional, you'll at the very last stage increase, yet again, your professional worth. All it takes is

understanding the unspoken rules, believing in
yourself, and not selling yourself short.

Part Two Establishing Your Professional Worth

NEVER SURRENDER YOUR POWER OVER YOU

I worked for an amazing company with a strong brand and an enormous fan base. Despite the challenges and difficulties I faced there, I am grateful for everything that the company provided me from life lessons to valuable skills that have benefited both my personal and professional life. This is the attitude I carry with me. Sincere and genuine gratitude. I learned real-world skills, and I learned how to be a leader, from which there is no going back.

I mastered time management, mastered the multifaceted practice of strong communication skills, especially non-defensive communication. I also discovered that I love coaching and mentoring others in a new way. I learned how to establish and command my professional worth, and I met my wife there as well.

One of the company's values, which they stood behind in practice, was integrity. But not everyone who worked there represented the positive aspects of the company. In fact, some people I worked with and worked for, I would feel contented never meeting again.

The company stood true to its values and principles. Who was at fault—the company or those who weren't aligned with them? After all, who you end up working with isn't always reflective of the organization as a whole or what they stand for.

Concerning proving myself, getting equal pay, and being rewarded for my merits, I was often on my own. But, as I mentored those who were marginalized and helped actualize their ambitions, my support base grew.

Despite the challenges I faced, I am truly grateful for all I learned and all the company gave me. I maintain contact with many of my old coworkers, whom I still consider close friends. At one point, I considered going back to the company. Keep in mind, I'd held a few other management positions with other companies since I left. And, after moving to the East Coast, I was at a crossroads with my career. So, I considered it, reflecting on my experiences through rose-colored glasses.

With an old boss's consent and a letter of recommendation, I applied for a position with the company on the East Coast. I went through three interviews with the manager of a local branch. This person seemed nice initially. And, in every interview, they expressed they were experiencing a shortage of supervisors, and pushed for me to apply for that position instead. But, I repeatedly expressed that I couldn't commit to that. I had other priorities in my life at that time, which required all my energy and focus.

When we touched on salary, they said they were prepared to offer me a set figure. However, my old boss advised me to advocate for my old wage. So, when I countered, they smiled wryly, and said they would have to have that approved by their regional. They then asked me if I wanted them to do that. I thought that was strange. So, I asked if it would hurt to ask, and they said no, and that it wouldn't be a problem. And, they explained, unless I heard from them, I should show up to work the following week. Then, they sent me home with my onboarding materials. I didn't hear anything, so I showed up at work.

I was given a tour with another new hire. I talked shop with the supervisor who oriented us. Then two hours later they showed up–two hours late for their shift–and they pulled me aside, saying they needed to talk to me for a minute, and we stepped outside. This is when they claimed they tried to reach me but they couldn't because they didn't have my phone number.

This person then explained they couldn't pay me at my old rate unless I came on as a supervisor, which I'd already expressed I couldn't commit to at that time. This person then explained the wage I was initially offered was the rate they pay a new supervisor. So, since I wasn't taking the supervisor position, they couldn't pay me more than that. Yet, what they told me next shocked me. They claimed they now could only hire me on at a wage lower than their initial offer.

I expressed confusion and attempted to clarify and mirror what they were saying, and whether they were indeed now offering a wage lower than their initial offer. They repeated the information, but this time offered an even lower wage than minutes before. I was baffled, confused, and had trouble understanding their behavior. Suddenly, all the memories of the negative experiences I had working for the company flooded my mind.

I found myself in an embarrassing situation. I was already there. Over the last two hours, I'd introduced myself and shook hands with over two dozen team members. I filled out new hire paperwork and now had to decide whether I was going to accept a wage far lower than what she'd initially offered.

I didn't operate like this, so I needed time to process and comprehend what was going on. Instead of making a knee-jerk decision, I opted to give them the benefit of the doubt. Subsequently, we entered the premises where they used the company laptop to complete the new hire paperwork alongside me. Then, as they filled out the field for my starting wage, they plugged in the wage I earned when I last worked at the company. They left that on the screen for about five seconds, then they slowly backspaced and entered the wage they'd initially offered me. Turning to me, they spoke in baby talk, asking, *"What did we agree upon?"* And put in the much lower wage. *"That's it. Yay! You did it!"* They smiled with their mouth, but not their eyes.

My face flushed. I felt humiliated and realized they were abusing their power. I now knew what kind of person they were, and their brand of leadership. This was indeed who I was going to be working for. After the onboarding, I went home and came to terms with my next move. That was when I texted them and rescinded my acceptance of their offer of employment.

> *"After taking some time to process our last encounter, I have decided to rescind my acceptance of your offer of employment. It is not an issue of the offered wage, which I ultimately consider to be generous, but rather for how the situation as a whole was handled. Your 'failed efforts' to reach me prior to on-boarding I found confusing, for you had successfully contacted me by phone for our prior two meetings. The manner and timing of your counteroffer of wage-waiting with the other new hire, post tour, with my belongings in the break room-placed me in an awkward and uncomfortable position. Intended or not, this felt disrespectful of my time.*

> *Lastly, I feel our last meeting was not entirely honest, for the specifics of that conversation were notable and left no room for confusion-and begs to question both meetings seeming similarly consistent in their changing narrative. I am a firm believer that for whatever reason people inform you who they are right off the bat. This is not the work environment I envisioned myself returning to, so I want to thank you for your offer of employment and generous offer of wage, which I would have gladly accepted with gratitude. I countered on the wage as a promise to several old superiors in the company. It is regretful that these circumstances unfolded as they did. I wish you the best of luck in all your endeavors."*

I dodged a bullet, and know with assurance I wouldn't have been happy working for that person. There have been multiple occasions where I bumped into them since that day. Each time, I held my head high, and they hung their head low. They revealed their true colors. Working for them would have been an unhappy experience and my self-respect would have eroded.

It won't matter how you quantify your professional worth, if you don't hold yourself to it. And, as soon as you allow someone to have power over you, to break you down, and to dictate your value to you, that's all you will be worth.

Instead, I was able to look in a mirror, look myself in the eye, and hold my head high. This is what happens when you are authentic and true to yourself. But it isn't always situationally easy. We weren't in a financial position at that time to turn down work. It was a difficult period.

Luck is where you find it. But you have to be on the lookout for luck; otherwise, you'll walk right by it without recognizing such opportunities. My luck was that they couldn't help but tell me who they were, and when that truth was revealed, I was able to walk away with courage and self-respect.

Everything in section one of this book was laid out to prepare you for what we'll cover in section two. We're going to provide greater insight into who your audience is, what their motives are, the stakes involved for them, and how you can make their job easier. You'll discover recruiter secrets, their motives, and how to leverage their questions to your advantage.

Throughout part two, we are going to focus on exactly this. We'll cover how to ensure the organization you are soliciting for employment is the right fit. Delving into the opportunities that can be gained from working together, we will assess whether the sacrifices are worth it. Also, we'll help you decide whether any job is the right opportunity for you as you continue through the interview process.

This section focuses on living with self-respect, making choices that suit you, getting the wage you deserve, setting clear expectations, staying true to your worth, and considering the big picture, and exactly what that big picture looks like.

Chapter 4
Who Are They &
What Do They Want?

I look at the pre-application process as preparing for a series of exams. If you do everything which was detailed in section one of this book, your written materials will receive a good grade when reviewed, and you'll move on to your oral exams. This is where the recruiter will test you on everything pertaining to you, and how it relates to them.

Since you're unaware of the tester's demeanor or bias, you'll want to come prepared. Preparing in advance will equip you with a better understanding of how you can appeal to your audience.

Long before your interview, you want to start asking yourself some serious questions when looking for the right job. Questions such as:

✦ Do I want to work here?

✦ Is this the right move for my career?

✦ Will this help or hurt my work-life balance?

You also need to question everything you learn along the way. By thoroughly researching each organization, you'll become increasingly skilled at anticipating and responding to their potential interview questions.

CONTROLLING BIAS

Pre-internet, being stalked was a frightening ordeal. Now, with the internet pervasive, everyone is a stalker to some extent. And you can count on every recruiter stalking you as soon as they receive your materials.

Once the interviewer examines your resume and cover letter, they will naturally want to delve deeper into getting to know the real you. They'll search for you online, browse your social media, and attempt to establish bias.

You see, social categorization is a common need among humans, being a tribal species. By categorizing others, and forming bias and stereotyping, a person decides whether you belong in other social groups or belong in theirs.

So, either set your social media visibility to private or for friends only, or make sure that your social media presence is professional and reflects you well. Also, if you've put your street address on your resume or cover letter, remove it! That recruiter might look up your house and form a bias against you based on the neighborhood you live in, or your residence, or the car in the driveway. Such bias might even alter what they offer you in pay. So, just put your name, email address, professional social media link, phone number, and the city you live in.

WHO IS INTERVIEWING WHO?

As I mentioned in section one, you want to keep what you present original. This includes your answers to their questions. You want to avoid being redundant, reiterating the same answer to various questions, and overly repeating points you've already made. For example, when your kitchen sink bio comes into play, you want to present original information on who you are as a professional and how your career journey led you here. It's your elevator pitch to get their attention, and is delivered when your interviewer asks one of the first questions of your interview:

✦ What can you tell me about yourself?

I'm sure you've heard the saying that *you are interviewing them as well.* This is more true than you know. Ask them the same questions they'd ask you. Think of the organization's value propositions, especially those on their website, which are aimed at recruiting their target talent. This is their version of their resume and cover letter. These are their materials designed to attract their ideal candidates. So, ask questions based on *your* motives.

✦What can you tell me about the organization, aside from what's on the website and social media?

Then ask yourself how well the recruiter represents that organization and their materials. Are they the same or in contradiction?

Feel free to ask important questions during the later part of the interview. It's your choice how assertive you want to be. But first, gauge the room. If things seem to be going well, ask specific questions that will help you decide if it's the right fit.

✦I couldn't find anything on these subjects online. Would you say that the organization is a meritocracy, or would you say tenure and seniority are prioritized over merit?

✦Do you have pay transparency?

✦What is the average pay rate among women compared to men?

✦I've read your DEI statements and the organization's accomplishments. What area of the organization holds the greatest balance of equality and diversity, and how does this department compare?

These are all valid questions. An organization that meets these qualifications will proudly answer them. An organization that doesn't might grow defensive when answering such questions, and you might not land a second interview. So, whether you want to ask these questions is up to you. But, in every interview, the recruiter is trying to determine whether the candidate sitting across from them is the right fit, and whether they would be a worthy investment. This is your goal as well. Taking this approach puts you in the power seat of your life and where you want to take it next. The choice is yours, regardless of whether it's the right choice.

AN ORGANIZATION'S IMAGE IS ONLY SKIN DEEP

Remember, a recruiting campaign is marketing with an agenda. Marketing is a form of propaganda, often integrating sociology and tribalism. So, pick apart their image. What is their aim? What are they after?

As you research each organization, from their website, code of conduct, media coverage, employee reviews, social media presence, or even talking to some of their employees, you'll have a clearer idea of what to expect from them.

Every finding should generate more questions. You'll want to examine their attention to these details. If they have poor employee reviews, what are they doing about those issues? How consistent is their performance? Do they offer enough opportunity for advancement from within? Are those opportunities aligned with your career goals? And are they likely to award those opportunities to you?

Just as you need to be consistent, so do they. If they are reliably empathetic and care about their employees' work-life balance, while offering generous maternity leave for both parents, making their value propositions actionable, you can probably trust they'll be consistent in what they offer. If they are reliably terrible, then count on them being terrible to you.

If they have a poor track record with offering equal pay between men and woman–unless women are earning more than men–you might want to seriously consider whether to pursue that opportunity. If you plan on having children, be cautious of organizations with a proven bias against maternity laws and regulations. As I mentioned before, a person reveals their true self from the start, and the same applies to organizations and their policies.

It's not uncommon for companies with terrible reputations to advertise monetary perks–such as great stock options–or offering promises for *getting rich quick*. When this is true, it's important to examine those poor employee reviews closely. Too often, such outfits use people up, burn them out, and indiscriminately fire them. So ask yourself whether that organization really is who they claim to be, and are they who you truly want to work for?

However, if you like them, and are excited by the idea of how that high-profile organization could catapult your career, and they stand by doing the right thing, go for it. But first and foremost, know yourself, be honest, and be calculated. You can assuredly count on them acting consistently according to the precedents they've set. And if they mistreat their employees, you will not be the exception.

As I have previously mentioned, luck is where you find it. Your future is the one that you picture yourself in. If you find an organization where everything feels right, and the opportunity is there, and you stand an equal chance at progressing your career, then pursue it.

Remember, when you are interviewing them, you need to focus on the details, and constantly ask yourself whether the person interviewing you truly embodies those values. All of these will help inform you of what it will be like to work with them.

QUESTIONS TO ASK YOURSELF THROUGHOUT YOUR RESEARCH & THROUGHOUT THE INTERVIEW

Sometimes your first interview might be with an AI assessment model, or by a third-party recruiter. Subsequent interviews will definitely involve an HR representative, or a supervisor, or a manager. Typically, the person interviewing you will be someone you'll collaborate with or report to. They represent both the working environment and the company. And three major tells can predict the work environment and advancement potential.

Communication-Do they communicate clearly and honestly? Or are they dodgy, and answer a question with a question? In the interview, do they seem like they are being deliberately confusing? If their communication skills aren't strong, or aligned with providing an honest answer to your questions, then this is what you can expect when advocating for your professional worth, for your career advancement, or other opportunities.

Expectations-Do they have realistic expectations, or do they offer tantalizing clues as to how difficult it will be working for them? If you remember, in Chapter Two, I shared an anecdote about a job I turned down. He was seeking a new manager to run his business. What he'd accomplished was impressive, and I admired what he'd built. I enjoyed meeting with him and his teams, and he'd almost sold me on taking the job. Then, as we were exiting our last interview, he told me who he was and turned the tables on himself. He warned me I would hate him. That's when I told him I needed some time to think about it.

We talked on the phone, and I explained I was accepting another offer. He circled back around a few times after that, offering me more and more money to come onboard. And the money was tempting. But I knew that if I took that job, he'd resent me for how much he had to spend to bring me on. And, as he warned me, I would hate him. He warned me I'd hate him if I took the job, and I believed him. And the money offered wasn't worth putting myself in a hostile work environment.

A Humanizing Work Environment-This one is important. Whether you will be afforded equal opportunity depends on how they treat their employees. Every company out there has DEI statements on their websites. Most of them generate reports quantifying how great and progressive they are. And all that equates to is propaganda–a self-aggrandizing poster they can put on the inside door to their break room, which makes it nothing more than cheap wallpaper. How do you know whether their statements are true? When in an interview, test their cultural competence. Ask them questions about their experience working in an equitable, diverse, and inclusive environment. How have those relationships they've built contributed to their individual success? How can you determine if they're being truthful when they answer those questions? Study their choice of words and their body language.

Someone who isn't open and doesn't embrace those values will lean back and increase their distance between themselves and the question. They might furrow their eyebrows, narrow their eyes, and avert their gaze. They might fold their arms across their chest, protect their neck with their hands, or in some other way become evasive and visibly uncomfortable. Or, someone who is comfortable discussing the subject, and is open and eager-culturally competent-will lean forward, soften their expression, raise their eyebrows, make eye contact, and express enthusiasm and pride in their tone, in their choice of words, and pride in the organization they work for.

Also, a company that has a high turnover rate, that showcases an elitist attitude, while speaking in dehumanizing terms about others, is less empathetic and less interested in increasing the skills of their workforce or in helping individual team members succeed. It signifies a workplace where weaknesses are exploited.

For example, *Supervisor A* understands that *Supervisor B* frequently embarks on inquisitions, and loves catching other people making mistakes, believing that doing so showcases their strong attention to detail. *Supervisor B* thrives on pointing out others' mistakes to make themself look better. This character flaw is *supervisor B's* weakness.

Let's say this scenario focuses on a subordinate employee with a learning disability. This employee is struggling to keep up. The pervasively authoritarian leadership style of that work environment has been hard on this employee, and they've grown increasingly rattled and in their perpetuated state of stress, they fumble more and are nervously making even more mistakes than before.

So, instead of modifying their leadership style to go the distance in helping that employee sharpen their skills, *Supervisor A* exploits the *Supervisor B's* weakness, and *Supervisor B* exploits that employee's weakness to get them fired. Here, everyone is set up for failure.

A humanized work environment focuses on caring for and supporting their people. They promote their strengths and thereby usher in a better work environment, which boosts their culture, creates a better brand, and greater innovation. This often results in a stronger client or customer experience.

Look past seeing what you want to see, pay attention to the details, and keep asking questions–inwardly or out loud. Asking your interviewer as many non-defensive questions about their work environment can help determine whether this is an employer who is truly aligned with your goals and will offer you the opportunity you are seeking. Ask how they would define the leadership style they promote in their organization. And brush up on differing leadership styles in advance. Such as transformative, influencer, coaching, transactional, democratic, bureaucratic, autocratic, laissez-faire, etcetera. Determining their leadership style is key to gauging your compatibility and potential for success.

Defining The Professional Relationship

It's up to you to define what your next professional relationship looks like. The organization should seem attractive in every way. You should decide for yourself whether they are who they say they are, and whether you trust them. What can they offer you? Do they feel like the right fit? Can they give you what you want?

Remember, even though they are paying you, unless you agree to a binding contract, you are free to walk away anytime. They may employ you, but does this make you their employee? Is that possessive appropriate? Or are you, by choice, entering a professional relationship?

They must, according to your rights and employee laws, have grounds for firing you beyond the evaluation period. You hold all the power in this relationship and are able to exit at will and without explanation. But there are consequences to acting rashly. It's often unadvisable to quit before securing another job... unless you planned for it. Maybe you recognized that the job demands were hindering your focused efforts to find the right opportunity. So, you saved enough money to sustain yourself for a few months, intentionally quitting before securing another job in order to search for the right one.

You retain complete power over yourself, and you maintain both your self-worth and your professional worth.

QUALITY OF LIFE

What can they offer and how can they incentivize you to join? Are they the right fit for you? Would working for them in that position increase your professional worth in your industry? Is their work environment conducive to your requirements for job satisfaction, or would it cause you to burn out? Let's say you are in a bind, and you need a job right now. So, what does it mean to take a job with a company that has a poor reputation? Their employee reviews state that their work environment is demoralizing. Yet, the job description states their environment is high-pressure and fast-paced. You might rationalize that this job only equates to a paycheck, and there are likely two sides to every story. Yet, the truth lies in the middle.

That work environment is likely to stress you out, to impact your morale, your psyche, your health, your sleep, and your personal life and relationships negatively. So, when you subtract the cost to your quality of life, is that paycheck worth it? Especially when you're losing out and stalling your career?

If you are salary springboarding, ask yourself why. Be honest with your motives and scrutinize whether it's truly worth it. If you see yourself as a short-term employee vying for a long-term opportunity, reconsider. Examine that decision from every angle, including how it might be perceived by a recruiter, who has a keen eye for spotting someone who salary springboards, and may be less likely to hire them.

HOW TO GET YOUR FOOT IN THE DOOR EVEN IF THEY'RE NOT HIRING

Reach out. If your preferred organizations aren't hiring, contact the hiring authority or HR. Explain that you would love to learn more about the organization, and would be interested in having a soft interview, or at the very least to take up some of their time to ask several questions. And, if they were willing to hang on to your resume, maybe they'll reach out when something comes available.

Prepare for that interview. Be willing to accept an internship and negotiate the terms. Be friendly, confident, and assertive. Show that you are hungry for an opportunity to work for them. Then, wait. Place yourself in a position where you are still working for your present organization, taking advantage of every opportunity to advance your career goals. And, if that opportunity you are waiting for requires you to adjust your career goals and pass some specific milestones that are aligned with them, strive to surpass them, and to be ready when that call comes through.

Don't put all your eggs in one basket. It's easy to get emotionally invested in the idea of any future. But the disappointment can sometimes be devastating. That's why you want to reach out to *every* organization that feels well aligned. In most circumstances, who you are applying to will tickle the recruiter's curiosity, and they'll ask what other companies you are soliciting. They'll want to assess the commonalities between your top choices and how they fit in.

When you share that list with them and who you are talking to, this will increase their stake in wanting to hire you. They might want to avoid a bidding war to employ you and try to hire you quickly.

THE RECRUITING PROCESS

You've learned everything you can about yourself, about their organization, and their employees. You've possibly even learned the name of the person you are interviewing with, and likely stalked them online, and maybe even connected with them on professional social media channels. So, what's left to accomplish before you land that interview?

Understand what went into attracting their ideal candidates to their talent pool.

It's the recruiter's job to evaluate which of their recruiting efforts are the most and least successful, so that they can narrow their focus and save the organization money in the future. So come prepared to help and explain what specifically drew you to this opportunity, and which recruitment marketing made the biggest impression.

Recruiting is expensive, nuanced, and high-pressure. The recruiter is not only responsible for attracting top performers but also responsible for screening out unqualified candidates. They are tasked with protecting the organization's assets and finding the right hire *right away*. You see, an organization's assets aren't limited to their finances and budget. An organization's assets are also each member of their teams and their morale. Other assets include their reputation and their ability to fulfill their promise to those they serve. Their employee retention rate is also a major asset.

Hiring an unqualified candidate will fatigue the rest of the team, without alleviating the burden of being short staffed. The onboarding and training depletes their payroll budget, burdens administration, and an unqualified candidate will probably render the position vacant yet again, restarting the entire recruiting process, which further exhausts the payroll budget.

When the recruiter is successful in their job and hires an ideal top-performing candidate sooner rather than later, the payroll budget they preserved can now be dedicated towards bonuses and pay incentives as a reward for the team's hard work. Hiring the right person also reflects well on the recruiter and boosts their reputation for team building and promoting the organization's culture.

Their job and their reputation depend on finding who they are looking for, and they can't find them unless they can get everyone to be sincere and honest with their answers. This requires some acrobatics. And remember, their one aim is to get to know who you are as a person and as a professional. When they ask each question, there's only one answer they want to hear: the truth.

The more you understand a recruiter's responsibilities and the risks behind every hiring decision, the more you'll appreciate their hard work. So, once you're versed on the context and attitude you wish to present your narrative with, and you've practiced your demeanor and accrued your confidence, approach the recruiter–your colleague–with appreciation, respect, empathy, and do everything you can to make their job easier.

Go into your interview with an appreciation for your audience. Familiarize yourself with how their business works–with an understanding of how much they can afford to pay you, along with any other offerings or incentives they might offer. Showcase that you have a *partner's scope* of the big picture. Being prepared and informed will add to your perceived professional worth and positively influence the bias of the hiring authority that you are appealing to.

Chapter 5
How To Deliver a Great Interview

THE COMPONENTS OF YOUR PERCEIVED VALUE

It's sometimes necessary to *fake it until you make it.* But even then, you first need to believe that you are who you say you are. And that person is who you have been all along. Your worth is in the eye of the beholder, and that eye is yours. This all starts with your self-perception, and perception is reality.

Remember, your interviewer is only interested in getting to know the real you. If you are trying to tell them what you *think* they want to hear, and you're being insincere or disingenuous, it will backfire. If you are having trouble convincing yourself that you have a great deal to offer, then go back and revisit your CV. Examine all that data you compiled that quantifies your worth. That data measurably exemplifies, through a clearly defined narrative, and through clear, transparent communication, that you are who you say you are.

When you're motivated by the work you enjoy, you are a reliable top performer. When that work you love to do is aligned with an organization you are interviewing with, you'll earn their trust, which increases your appeal. Your interest in potentially engaging in a long-term professional relationship with them, and your interest in their training, developmental opportunities, their brand, and their approach all contribute to your perceived value as a potential asset. Showcasing a strong work ethic by arriving at your interview informed, prepared, rehearsed, and with the right attitude actionably communicates that you are a top performer.

Meditating on, contextualizing, and being able to communicate your professional journey, your worldview, and your goals with clarity puts you in full control of your narrative. Understanding the job of the recruiter, understanding the needs of the business, and coming equipped with clear and realistic expectations of how you and the organization can meet each other's needs increases your professional worth.

And, informing them of what you aim to accomplish, and what you hope to gain, and in clearly definable terms, what they can do to help you get there, also increases your professional worth.

VERBAL & NON-VERBAL CUES

There are several nuances to communication, and both your verbal & non-verbal communication skills will impact your professional worth.

Written Communication-Being adept at the written word simply requires conveying information in a manner that's easy to read.

Verbal Communication-This pertains to how effective you are at ensuring the message you aim to send is actually the message that is received. When communicating orally, the meaning and emotional intent can be conveyed through volume, speed of speech, pauses, and speech crutches. Then, there's your tone and your choice of words, which also communicate your attitude, bias, and worldview, which conveys the negative or positive emotional intent of your messaging.

Non-Verbal Communication-This wordlessly accompanies what one says. For example, someone asks you to share a situation where you experienced a conflict at work, and you reflexively lean back, creating distance between you and the person who triggered a negative association. You furrow your brow, narrow your eyes and cradle your neck with your hands or fold your arms across your chest.

This body language communicates that recalling the event triggered an emotional response such as feelings of defensiveness and discomfort. This implies you still haven't reconciled or learned from it, and you felt victimized. These are all signs of unreliability and a lower degree of emotional intelligence. It suggests a lack of growth and a low tolerance for stress. It also could suggest underdeveloped mediation, diplomacy, and non-defensive communication skills.

Alternatively, when asked that same question, imagine you softened your face and leaned forward in your chair, legs apart and hands relaxed on your knees. Softly smiling, you made eye contact and shared the details, including the key players and how you improved communication and de-escalated the situation to a successful outcome. You then expressed how conflict is integral to innovation and you always welcome being challenged.

In this scenario, you've nonverbally communicated that you are self-assured, professional, strong, exhibit situational leadership skills, and possess a high EQ. This response increases your professional worth.

Yet, to truly showcase your skills, you'll want to interview them on these same points. Inquire about their team dynamic, the ways in which their teams challenge each other, and ask about the personalities you would potentially work with, should all parties agree to move forward through the next stages of the interview process.

Lastly, it's important to practice delivering your answers before your interview, making sure you avoid using any speech crutches or ticks, such as compulsively using the word "*like*," or saying "*um*" or "*ah*" rather than just pausing.

The more clearly and eloquently you speak throughout your interview, the more you will be considered a strong communicator capable of meeting the demands of the job.

NON-DEFENSIVE COMMUNICATION

You may have practiced this concept before. You may even be a master of it. But for those unfamiliar, the trick to non-defensive communication is focusing on the situation and not the person. When addressing a situation, you need to observe it from a bird's-eye view. As soon as you single out or inadvertently assign blame to an individual, you will probably trigger a defensive response, and the conversation will dissolve into finger-pointing, justification, positioning, and conflict. If no growth opportunities are identified, the matter will not improve, and relations are strained.

Let's imagine something unplanned arises, and suddenly the job at hand becomes more difficult. Amidst this stress, an employee who has been facing personal challenges struggles with the stress of this situation and expresses frustration. They're essentially communicating that they won't be able to meet expectations.

So, you step in and empathize and agree that *"the situation is unfortunate. But if everyone can act fast in a coordinated fashion and work smarter, it isn't unrealistic to accomplish what needs to be done under the deadline. But it will take acting fast to make that happen."*

This is great non-defensive communication. But if you were to come forward and say, *"I need you to calm down."* Talking in a confrontational manner like this won't help. It will only waste your precious time while showcasing your poor interpersonal skills and poor leadership skills.

Non-defensive communication never points fingers. It examines a situation and says, *"I think I see what happened here."* Being a strong communicator means going the distance. It is about being patient, wise, and willing to listen, to mirror the other person's concerns, while validating them and making sure they've felt heard and empathized with.

When a situation is presented from an impartial aerial view, all viewpoints are considered. It requires leaning in with friendly confidence and transparency, while holding yourself accountable every step of the way. This showcases a high EQ, leadership potential, patience, wisdom, and strong interpersonal skills.

YOUR INTERVIEW ENVIRONMENT

Whether you are in a live interview, a video interview, or taking a prerecorded interview conducted by an AI-driven assessment model, you'll want to be careful what you communicate non-verbally. Bias is everywhere, especially when concerning artificial intelligence. And just like with people, the AI assessment model may easily misinterpret your non-verbal cues and eliminate you from moving further through the recruiting process.

Most assessment models are designed to behaviorally analyze your facial cues. So ensure your face has natural and even lighting during a video interview. Avoid fluorescent light, or being lit from below, and most especially avoid being backlit. Without seeing your face, your interview may not be forwarded to a live recruiter.

Your surroundings will also be evaluated for how organized your workspace is. So make sure your surroundings are distraction-free, and that your setting is professional and presentable. Be sure to let everyone in your residence know you are going into an interview and that you need silence.

Also, showcase that you are well-prepared when it comes to any undertaking. Use the restroom before your interview begins. Have a glass of water ready. Silence notifications, ensure you have a strong Wi-Fi signal, and make sure you have no issues with the interview portal by familiarizing yourself with how it works well in advance.

BUILDING TRUST

A recruiter needs to gain an understanding of how you'll fit into their teams. A recruiter is in effect a team builder. And the teams they build need to fit their culture, which embodies their brand. So, one of the most important tasks they need to accomplish is deciding how well you'll fit their mold, including how well you'll get along with the current members of their teams.

Whether you can be trusted, and how well you'll fit into their teams will depend on your approach to onboarding, and how effectively you go about establishing relationships with your peers. Additionally, your approach to proving yourself, earning your keep, and how you contribute are all of equal importance and directly influence how you'll fit in.

For example, someone who doesn't put in the time to understand fully how things work and quickly starts coming up with ideas for how to do things better will accomplish many things, and not all of them are desirable. For starters, it shows an eagerness to contribute and an appreciation for being awarded the position. But it also shows a lack of respect for what more tenured employees already built. It shows an arrogance and presumption that things need fixing. They don't take the time to understand why those systems are in place. They don't ask questions and are crudely ambitious. It also reveals they're solely interested in advancing their own goals with little regard for their teams.

So how do you establish trust, earn respect, build relationships, and actively contribute? Work both smart and hard. Be open, transparent, bounded, and honest with everyone. Ask each teammate questions and for their insight and advice. Keep what others share with you to yourself unless it violates the organization's code of conduct, goes against their values, or compromises assets.

Earn the trust of your teams by actively listening. All it takes is being open and empathetic while expressing genuine curiosity. Study the way things are done, and when making a suggestion, go in with the presumption that it may have been tried or suggested before. This is how you can contribute, innovate, and most importantly, learn and grow.

Someone entrusted with increasing responsibility is a stakeholder in the group's success. So you'll want to earn trust by trusting others, to go above and beyond helping your peers, and to rise up and volunteer. Build relationships through humility, leaning on your teams, and giving credit where credit is due. Taking this approach increases visibility, which leads to recognition and an ever-expanding professional network.

NAVIGATING WORKPLACE POLITICS

There are rules to the game of workplace politics, and nearly 100% of those rules are unspoken. And, like chess, there are endless ways you can play the game. It's my belief that you should always play the game according to your brand of sports-womanship–for lack of a better term–in accordance with your own nature.

Numerous external factors–such as job market conditions–can impact you positively or negatively. But, the perception of being in demand is within your control. All that takes is the right mindset and a strategic approach. Simply by mastering the art of humble confidence, rather than arrogant cockiness, you'll become a true samurai in the work-politics arena.

Workplace politics is like dancing–navigating the political arena without stepping on any toes. Understanding, and practicing, the rules, in a chess master fashion, will make navigating workplace politics a reflex, done blindly, and will detract nothing from you, while ever preserving your self-respect.

In fact, when adept and equipped with how workplace politics work, and playing them according to your own rules and nature, you reveal you can be trusted, can promote the bottom line, which also increases your professional worth.

MAKING IT THROUGH EACH INTERVIEW ROUND

How effectively you communicate and answer each question will influence others' perception of your professional worth. This will dictate whether you qualify for a second or a third interview. Additionally, you'll likely be interviewed by more than one person, together or separately. You'll therefore have to appeal to each new person you interview with, staying fresh yet consistent, without being redundant. And, each new person you interview with offers opportunities to fill in the gaps of what life working there will look like.

To ensure the consistency of your performance, be mindful of what they are trying to determine about you. They want to know how your behavior will impact your workplace relations and the ability to collaborate with their teams. They want to know how consistent your performance and attitude are, and how reliable of an employee you'll be.

They want to know what accomplishment and success look like to you, while scaling it against your mode of going above and beyond. Lastly, they want to determine if you are who you say you are, and whether you are who they are seeking. These are the core elements of your performance indicators.

Now, if everything here feels well aligned, they'll want to determine whether they can afford to hire you, or whether they can afford to pass you by. Are you priced out of their pay range or are you such a valuable asset that they stand to benefit by paying you more? They'll weigh these questions against whether you would be a short-term versus a long-term hire, and whether they think they can keep you motivated on the job.

There are a few factors that can impact their decision. Namely, how actively you are interviewing elsewhere, whether you are looking to work for an organization similar to theirs, and whether you have received any competing offers, such as your current employer making you an offer to stay onboard with them.

To deliver fresh and meaningful responses without being redundant from one interview to the next, do what you can to understand each person you interview with, including the job they have to perform, and arrive at each interview equipped with fresh and insightful questions for each person.

Also, remember, the aim isn't just to wow them with how original and forward-thinking you are. Your primary aim is to convince them you are the right person for the job. Learn everything you can about them and their organization to determine your fit, the opportunity they offer, how working with them will increase your professional worth, and whether you even want to work for them.

HOW TO AVOID
A CARROT & STICK CAREER PROGRESSION

One of the primary questions you'll be asked in an interview will be

✦ Where would you like to take your career with our company?

Failing to answer this question successfully, without clearly setting expectations for how they can advance your career goals, will come at a great future cost to your development.

Most people answer with,

✦ *"I could see myself maybe at some point moving up into a supervisor position."*

This answer doesn't establish clear training timelines, training intensity, the department you'd ideally like to advance into, or your desired promotion timeline. Rather, it gives them carte blanche to offer you an empty incentive. This is the carrot they will continually motivate you with, allowing them to push you harder without providing any proper reward. It allows them to make excuses for why you haven't been awarded that opportunity yet, holding you to a higher work standard than your current pay grade. You'll be doing the job of a supervisor without being paid for it, and held accountable to unrealistic expectations.

Now imagine–after they ask you where you would like to take your career with their company–that you pull out your career plan detailing how you've incorporated the opportunities they advertise on their company website. Your plan details how their value propositions–such as how they suggested *rising-leaders* can join their mentorship program–appealed to you. You share your desire to grow, your capacity to learn, while showcasing your leadership potential. You suggest you'd like to have a mentor assigned to you within six months, for your aggressive training to begin in 8 months, and to be promoted to a supervisory position within 15 months, or 18 at the very latest.

With these clearly mapped-out time-lined milestones, you'll set clear expectations. Whether this ends up being a short- or long-term employment opportunity solely depends on whether they can keep you motivated by giving you what you want–a mentorship, coaching, training, added responsibilities, additional skills, and eventually a more respected title.

Not only are you avoiding a carrot-and-stick career progression, but you've negotiated, from the outset, an opportunity to advance beyond your peers, to accomplish a great deal with their company, and negotiated being rewarded with trust and increased stake in the success of the organization, while earning greater pay through merit.

Now, once they've invested their resources into you, you'll be in a better position when you eventually consider leaving the company. This ultimately will result in it costing them more to replace you than to continually advance both your skills and your rank in the company.

But curtailing a carrot-and-stick career progression doesn't stop there. The key rule for receiving awards based on your merits is to not be stealthy in your work. In other words, be a samurai, not a ninja.

Be careful though, for when they ask you how you like to be motivated, avoid suggesting that financial perks motivate you, as you'll only be advertising that you are only in it for the money, and motivated by little else. This implies a lack of loyalty and a willingness to switch sides for better offers, leaving them in a bind.

BE CLEAR ON WHAT YOU WANT

When delivering interview coaching advice, I can't tell you the number of times a person I was consulting told me they were planning to demand a lot of money when it came time to negotiate their pay. They'd rationalize:

✦ They make a lot of money as a business, so they can afford to pay more.

Every time I hear this, my reaction remains unchanged, leading into a familiar conversation I've had with many individuals.

Just because a company seems successful from the outside doesn't mean they have an unlimited payroll budget. That's not how a business works. And advertising ignorance about how a business functions dramatically lowers your professional worth. Why would they pay you more when another candidate with similar qualifications is willing to get paid less? This almost always leads to the following questions:

✦ How do I know how much to ask for?

✦ What is the most they can pay me?

✦How can I get them to pay me for my perceived professional worth?

Before your interview, make a list of everything they can provide, or that which you can barter that will ultimately increase your professional worth over time. By setting expectations clearly from the onset, you'll avoid a carrot and stick career progression. You might negotiate terms for working remotely in a hybrid work environment. You might negotiate working on-site in exchange for a corner office. Or, you might advocate for child care assistance, or to eventually transfer to one of their other global offices, or being able to bring your dog with you to work.

Other questions you'll want to ask when discussing salary are whether tenure is preferred over experience and merit, and whether they would refer to their work culture as a meritocracy. Or, whether they offer pay transparency, are willing to disclose the difference in percentage men earn versus women, and statistically how many women are in leadership positions in their company versus men. You might also want to determine what kind of availability they require, and whether performance is closely monitored or whether they trust their employees to be self-managed in their work.

What is your loyalty worth, and what will your loyalty offer your career advancement? If they ask you to relocate or travel for work, how will that impact your quality of life, and what is that worth to you? If navigated correctly, just by setting these attainable terms, you've yet again increased your professional worth. You need to want what you are asking for.

You are basically showcasing you are a true professional and informing them of the price of your loyalty. Remember, when entering into a new professional relationship, it's a business relationship. When discussing business, it's important to discuss price.

Remember, the employee is always in the power position. They have the upper hand, and more rights, while labor laws restrict every employer. So, set your terms. Be realistic and come equipped with an understanding of whether they can accommodate your terms.

IMPROVE YOUR SALARY NEGOTIATION GAME

The more adeptly you can answer every question will contribute to your professional worth. Whenever you're asked about salary expectations, avoid giving them a direct answer. Doing so quickly closes negotiations. So before ever discussing numbers, you need to better understand their perception of your worth, and what they can afford to offer, which extends beyond pay rate or salary.

You see, professional worth can be increased through the accrual of skills, title, and your portfolio or connections throughout your industry–which adds to your value in the eyes of headhunters. But when answering salary-based questions, you need to equip yourself with some important figures in advance.

PUT A NUMBER ON IT

First, calculate the time-cost and expense-cost of your commute. Put a number on it. Leave nothing on the table. We're talking about public transportation costs–or the cost of petrol, maintenance, insurance, and wear and tear on your car–and the time it takes to commute. If you drive, factor in not only the distance in miles, but traffic congestion at commuter hour, how much time out of your week is spent fueling your gas tank, washing your car, getting oil changes, etcetera. Your time is money. If they offer commuter benefits, look at how that offsets those costs.

Then consider any wellness expenses, such as gym memberships, behavioral health, physical health, and insurance, and whether you'll be salary or hourly, and how that will impact whether you can leave your work behind or are expected to take it home with you.

Compare their benefits offerings with those provided by your present or previous employers. This issue is about cost of living and should have a dollar value. Then, get a fair understanding of their budget by asking several telling questions.

✦ How long has the job posting been up?

✦ How heavily have your extended recruiting efforts impacted your payroll budget?

✦ What does your projected payroll budget look like through the fiscal year?

Do you receive a yearly bonus? How frequently is your performance reviewed–once or twice a year–and how many of those reviews come with a potential pay increase? Map out not only what you are currently earning, but do the math to determine what your average pay increase percentage has been, year after year.

Separate every single thing you can think of, from current annual income, projected pay increase, benefits, expenses, to any other factors that impact your cost of living. Then compare their offerings to those figures. Another important question to ask is when their next performance reviews are, and if they include a pay increase for top performers, and whether you would qualify for a potential pay increase upon the next review period.

In summary, when asked what kind of salary you would like to earn, present your numbers and your understanding of their figures. Then, clearly define what you expect within a realistic range, taking into consideration where you are at in your career. Also detail where you'd like to take your career next and the direction you'd like to rise up within their company.

When you have competing offers, always give the other company a chance to counteroffer. It is also perfectly acceptable to take a day, or as much time as they'd allow, to consider each offer. And, each time, take only as much time as you need.

INTERVIEW PERFORMANCE TAKEAWAYS

It's crucial to examine, with heightened self-awareness, how you should rate each interview performance. You need to identify your growth opportunities as well as where you shined. You want to ensure you are an observer of the situation, rather than being governed by an emotional interpretation. If you didn't nail it, don't be too hard on yourself. Take it in stride and learn from the experience.

Always allow yourself some time to process how everything went, while maintaining confident, emotional equilibrium, from beginning to end. This ensures you are being compassionate and truthful to yourself. It also ensures that you don't reflexively react to any situation, but meditatively respond.

A CASE IN POINT

I once interviewed for a management position within a prestigious organization. The first interview went quite well. For starters, I answered every question with ease. I walked the walk, talked the talk, and got along with the person who was interviewing me smashingly. We hit it off, and I felt confident in my abilities and my prospects. At the end of the interview, we immediately scheduled the next round for the following week. In that next sit-down, I was going to meet with their manager, who I would also serve under if I landed the job.

Fast forward seven days and I sat down with both of them. From the start, the leading manager was abrasive, disrespectful, and demeaning towards their assistant manager. It was an uncomfortable situation, and I felt I was intruding in a hostile work environment where I didn't belong.

Shortly into the interview, the leading manager dismissed the assistant manager I'd previously interviewed with. The rest of our conversation was then amicable, yet I continually took note of their abrasive tone and curt behavior. In fact, it often seemed they went out of their way to come across as unimpressed by my accomplishments and disinterested in my responses to their interview questions.

Eventually, towards the end of the interview, they admitted they didn't have a business card with them, so they guided me through the building to their office. When we entered their office, I was shocked. In a completely disorganized manner, they had piles of papers stacked everywhere. The pathway to their desk was blocked by boxes of items, which were literally collecting dust. They even had a new meat grill, still in the box, behind their computer. I couldn't imagine getting anything done in a space like that. It was more reflective of a hoarder than a manager.

As the interview came to a close, we made small talk, and then the manager hurriedly shook my hand and sent me off. As I drove home, I considered how that experience was the antithesis of my first interview with that company. I saw how the manager treated their employees–not well–and how disorganized they were.

Grading that manager's interview performance, I would say they were underprepared, had a poor work-life balance, are likely governed by their emotions, and bring their personal issues and personal obligations to work with them. I would also say they are clearly disorganized, unprofessional, that they are not capable of communicating non-defensively, and under-performs with poor management skills and poor people skills.

Considering this, I had no interest in working for them. So, I later sent a brief email thanking them for their time and interest in meeting with me. And that was that. I didn't hear from them again, which mattered little.

As you interview, learn, grow, show appreciation, and move onwards and upwards. Go in with the right attitude and perspective. Post-interview, always weigh the implications of what working with them would look like. Be honest with yourself about what you want, what you learned, and whether they are capable of giving you what you want.

Next chapter, we'll deep dive into the most common interview questions you'll likely face and how to answer them.

Chapter 6
Controlling The Interview

So far, we've laid the foundation for your professional worth and how the way you carry yourself showcases your value. You're now clear in your mind whether that job is an opportunity worth pursuing. You are fully conscious of what you offer and what they stand to gain from hiring you. Also, you're now equipped with a cursory understanding of the recruiter's goals and motives and the commonalities you share.

In any interview, the key components are:
✦ To display that you are a stakeholder
✦ To display that you're a team player who is interested in growing with the team

✦ To reflect the mindset they look for in their ideal employees

Success in this mutual endeavor serves both your interests. You are learning what you need to know about each other. You share similar goals and face similar pitfalls. The more informed you both are, the more capably you'll both be able to make a calculated decision. A consensus must be reached. How coordinated your efforts are will better help you answer whether you'll be able to work together, or not work together.

Your goal is to maintain control of your narrative, to uphold the right attitude, and to present yourself as not only their target talent, but as a top-tier professional. Whereas, the recruiter's goal is to get to know who you are while maintaining control of the interview.

When a recruiter loses control of the interview, their own biases can render them vulnerable to being manipulated into making a poor hiring decision. In the long-term, this benefits no one.

On the other hand, if they have more to gain from hiring you than you have to gain from taking the job, it might not be the best fit for you. So, arrive as both an interviewee, fully prepared to answer any and all of their questions, and show up as an interviewer as well, determined to learn everything you can about the job.

ANTICIPATING AND ANSWERING THE RIGHT QUESTIONS

I always say that there are no trick questions when you already know the answers. However, there are tricky questions you can definitely count on in every interview. Some questions are designed to catch you off guard while testing how quickly you think on your feet. Other questions aim to probe, reveal, and expose your truths. Then there are simpler questions designed to test your technical skills, experience level, and how proficient you are in your field.

An interview is all about discovery. And, recruiters know the answers they'll get will be mostly unanticipated, sometimes prompting a new line of questions, especially when a candidate fumbles and volunteers too much information when caught underprepared.

Any time a question comes your way that catches you off guard or confuses you, give yourself permission to pause. Explain that you'd like to give that question the answer it deserves. In that moment, ponder which category that question belongs to. Allow yourself the time to respond with confidence, rather than reacting nervously and rashly, and delivering a rushed answer that betrays your narrative and raises an unintentional red flag.

BREADCRUMB QUESTIONS

There will be several questions where the answer is built into them. For example, if one of the organization's core values is to deliver a 'wow' customer service experience, and the interview question is:

✦ How would you define a wow customer service experience?

This is a test of how thoroughly you've prepared for your interview and whether you're familiar with their core values. If you didn't spend time researching their company and only came prepared to speak about your skills, your answer will reveal how you didn't prepare. They then won't think much of your work ethic, and won't be convinced you are interested in working specifically for them. Rather, they'll more likely think;

✦ Just because you need a job doesn't mean our company needs you.

SITUATIONAL & BEHAVIORAL QUESTIONS

These questions serve as a method for evaluating your emotional intelligence, and whether you have control over your stress, or whether you allow your stress to govern your responses, which can impact your reaction time. In other words, they assess your problem-solving skills, and whether you can react swiftly in high-pressure situations.

These questions are often presented as hypothetical situations that challenge you to describe your decision-making in real time. Or, they'll ask you to describe how you managed certain specific situations in the past.

The key to answering is to focus on assessing the risks involved in the presented situation, recalling how you reacted to comparable circumstances in the past, while providing examples when you maintained governance over your emotions and stress levels.

When questions such as these are posed, you'll want to stay calm, cool, and collected. If, when recalling your example, you find the previously experienced stress rises back to the surface, choose a different example to share.

Remember, stress is nearly always visible, and you'll want to remain conscious of your body language throughout your interview. So smile with confidence, try to remain calm, and be mindful of your body language at all times.

QUESTIONS TESTING YOUR COMFORT ZONE

Questions such as these are typical, each designed to assess how you react when an unanticipated question arises, forcing you outside of your comfort zone. Such as:

✦ What would your bosses say about you if I contacted them?

Your body language will potentially reveal how that question makes you feel. If you worry they might have already talked to your employer, and you stumble with your answer, that's saying a lot. Whereas if you seem confident and in your comfort zone, it attests to your credibility as a viable candidate.

✦ Are you open to traveling or relocating for work?

Suppose there was no indication of this job requirement. The answer distinguishes those who did their homework from those who didn't. It also stands to reveal how adaptable you are and how you react and respond in uncomfortable situations.

The key to answering this question is to showcase you have a high EQ by following up with clarifying questions. Such as:

✦ *"That's an interesting question. I did thoroughly research the company, their locations, and this role. It seemed that this position didn't require travel or relocation. Is this question purely hypothetical, or do you have a different position in mind that better suits my skills? I suppose I would take any future offers or requests under consideration if it felt like it was the right move to advance my career goals and ambitions."*

SIMILARLY PHRASED QUESTIONS

These questions sound alike, yet through clever wordplay are distinct. The question itself is a test of your attention to detail. Your answer will also potentially reveal how well you've prepared for the interview. For example, when an interviewer first asks:

✦ Why work for us?

Then follows up with,

✦ Why should we hire you?

It is a test of your communication skills. A redundant answer is a fail, and an original answer is a pass.

Similarly Phrased Questions also help distinguish the confident from the nervous. A common symptom of being nervous is trying to rush the interview and to try to hurry through it.

For example, a nervous person might answer question A–*Why work for us?*–with a pitch for hiring them. In doing so, they've given their answer to question B–*Why should we hire you?*–before it was asked, and not in the appropriate context. Then, when asked question B, they reiterate the same answer they've given to question A, and end up sounding redundant. They're visibly stressed and unable to focus on the details. They stumble over their words and come across as having poor communication skills.

Someone who's confident and prepared, and who has a slightly different agenda, remains calm, cool, and collected. They're engaged in the interview, fixated on getting all of their questions answered, and are focused on the details.

There is a right way to answer both questions.

Why work for us? Explain your motives for wanting to work for them, and how their organization and opportunity align with your goals.

Why should we hire you? Share who you are, your alignment with their culture, and why you admire the company.

The recruiters' note will look something like this:

✦ *"Original-thinks quickly on their feet-arrived prepared-strong work ethic-keen attention to detail-strong communication skills..."*

TIGHTROPE QUESTIONS

Early on I had a colleague tell me I was honest... to a fault. What he meant was that my honesty often stood in the way of my ambitions, especially when being completely transparent wasn't appropriate for the situation. In other words, this isn't necessarily a flaw, per se, as long as my honesty didn't betray the context of my narrative and obstruct my goals and ambitions. Even though a person's honesty is often reflective of their integrity, how boundaried or forthcoming someone is can offer insight into their experience level and naiveté.

Someone who isn't boundaried is honest to a fault. They overshare and are more likely to fail at tightrope questions. Tightrope questions are a balancing act. They test how focussed and how boundaried you are. For example, a common tightrope question is:

✦ If you could start your career over and take it in another direction, what would your ideal career path be?

Imagine you are a career manager, and you confess you would love to be an elementary school educator. That's nice, but it reveals you fell into your career rather than pursuing it by choice. This insinuates you are likely unhappy with the career you're in, and there are other career paths you would likely prefer to pursue. In other words, your heart isn't in your work. Providing such an answer makes you honest to a fault. But, as I have reiterated, it is the context that counts.

✦ *"I don't think I would change my career, not at all. You see, I used to think I aspired to be a teacher. However, I now often find myself coaching my teammates, educating them on how to work smarter while advancing their careers. So, nothing's changed, I am still educating and living according to my nature. If I had to choose, I might have just done a thing or two differently to further advance my career. But that's just hindsight talking. And the best thing about hindsight is that when you refocus hindsight towards the future, it transforms it into foresight."*

Your response was honest, focused, and you controlled your narrative in a way that benefits you. The key to walking a tightrope question is staying centered on the context of your narrative. Your narrative is your truth, and your attitude is the balancing pole that keeps you centered. This requires communicating intention with consistency.

QUESTIONS OPEN TO INTERPRETATION

These questions aim to reveal your perception of the world, which informs your attitude. For example:

✦ Tell me about the last time you experienced a conflict at work.

There are many ways this question can be interpreted. A conflict could imply a conflict of interest. It could also mean a conflict you mediated between two coworkers. Perhaps it could suggest a disagreement with a colleague you spearheaded a project with. Maybe you struggled to see eye to eye, but reached a consensus on how to approach the work. Or, it could mean a bareknuckle cage fight to the death over the last cup of coffee in the break room, or even confronting who ate your lunch.

These questions stand to reveal how a candidate interprets them.

✦ Tell me about a time you disagreed with your manager.

✦ Tell me about a time you disagreed with your company's policy.

There are various ways to answer these questions.

Someone who doesn't understand the nature of such a question might share an anecdote of when they challenged a supervisor openly in front of the team, primarily because they clashed with their personality or leadership style. Or, they called out an unpopular restructure or rebranding, spreading rumors that everyone's job security was at risk. Yet what does such an answer reveal?

Those answers suggest they don't get along with those in positions of authority. They are bridge burners rather than bridge builders. Job security concerns arise for under-performers during restructures or rebranding, typically out of a fear of their poor work ethic being exposed. It also suggests that instead of supporting their supervisor, or the team, or the company's messaging, they run with assumptions and sow dissent. So, using their answer as a predictor of future job performance, the recruiter will assume they are an under-performer and are not a team player. Lastly, they cannot be trusted to support the company's brand or vision.

Yet simply understanding the nature of the question can give you an opportunity to make yourself shine. For example:

✦ *"Well, after meeting to discuss a project, assignments were handed out. We were all discussing our roles. I realized our manager had forgotten about a particular skill set of mine, and I was better suited for those tasks assigned to my teammate. So, I suggested I swap duties with him. I believed I could expedite that portion of the project, finish it early, and then help out elsewhere, wherever needed. They were grateful I challenged them for the greater good, and for how I went about it. But, as I saw it, I was just anticipating need."*

FOLLOW-UP QUESTIONS

An interview is a dance. Remember, it's your interviewer's goal to get you to relax and be your unfiltered self. It's in their best interest to get to know the real you. So, when you lower your guard, do so strategically. Be friendly and open, but remain boundaried. Be honest, but not to a fault. And remember, you don't know them yet either, and getting to know them is your goal. So don't make assumptions, or fully trust the first impressions they're strategically aiming to make.

For example, when you let your guard down and overshare even just a little, your interviewer will probably hone in on it. When something you've said inspires them to dig deeper, they'll express interest in a non-defensive way, and when that happens, it should raise your antenna. You see, this is always a strong sign that you may have inadvertently raised a red flag. Take care of how you answer their line of questioning and maintain self-control and the context of your narrative. Never grow defensive, or backpedal, or contradict your previous answers. Just focus on the details and proceed with self-awareness and caution.

Then, when you reach the end of your interview, and your interviewer asks if there are any other questions they can answer for you, ask them something along these lines:

✦ I have several. But first, since we are still getting to know each other, I am curious if anything I have said or volunteered throughout this interview might have raised some more questions? Particularly anything you may have interpreted as a red flag, which I could now clarify or dispel for you.

Asking this tests their communication skills, persuades them to volunteer how they interpreted your answer, and gives you the strength position of taking back control of your narrative.

WHAT THE INTERVIEWER NEEDS TO KNOW

Every recruiter needs to look at a new hire as an investment. What they learn from your answers to their questions will typically inform them of how sustainable and reliable an employee you'd be. The less risky the investment, the better.

They need to know if you are truly the right fit for them—if your goals align with their opportunities, and if your brand aligns with theirs. The more talented, professional, and experienced you seem—with the right attitude, perspective, and big picture lens–the more that you'll be able to offer their organization.

Remember, ultimately, the interviewer needs to get to know who you are as a person and as a professional. On a personal level, they want to know how your attitude informs your world view and your decision-making. Are you truly the person you claim to be? Is how you present yourself now a reliable representation of who you are?

Self-awareness could be defined as the alignment between how one sees themself and how others perceive them. So they'll ask questions aimed at revealing how aligned your self-perception is with how others perceive you. For example, someone who is self-aware and eagerly looks for growth opportunities is someone who proactively seeks out feedback rather than waiting for it to come around to them.

The interviewer will also want to learn more about your emotional intelligence, the mistakes you've made and the failures you faced, and how you've dealt with them. They'll want to know whether you've learned from those experiences, and whether hiring you would present as a potential asset, as opposed to presenting as a risk or liability.

They are also looking for indications of where your true passions lie, whether you are prone to burn out on the job quickly, or are presently burned out in your career. They'll also want to know more about your work ethic and performance standard, and will aim to assess your answers for predictors of future job performance. This information can also be used to inform them of your development and growth potential. So, prepare for your interview. Find a mock interview site, such as MockQuestions.com, and practice out loud, recording your answers so you can get a firm perspective on how others might perceive you. Also, when performing mock interviews, explore various companies and industry question sets, and not just the company you're interested in.

There may also be questions which aim to inform them whether you are the type who leaves their previous employer on good or bad terms, and whether you are a bridge builder or someone who burns bridges behind you and never looks back. Someone who is a bridge builder is typically better at building relationships and has a firm understanding of what they offer and how they contribute to their teams. So, arrive equipped with references and letters of recommendation. Bring any documentation that backs up your claims of who you say you are.

WHAT YOU WANT THE INTERVIEWER TO KNOW

When I was employed by others—as opposed to presently being self-employed—I always viewed the primary function of my job, in its most distilled form, as making my superiors' jobs easier.

Taking time to understand the inner workings of the business makes you a stakeholder. The greater your interest in how you can contribute to the larger scheme of things—through active listening, anticipating need, and taking measures to understand the logic behind the decision-making of your superiors–the more of a valued investment you'll appear to be.

So, when they ask questions driving at what you could offer their company, this is what they're after. Telling them isn't enough. You have to display that you carry this mindset, and that you walk the walk and talk the talk. This means asking the right questions and showcasing an interest in the big picture, while viewing the job as a top performer would. Doing so makes your answers and statements actionable. It reveals the right mindset, which presents you as an asset. Taking this approach will raise you up higher than most of the other candidates they're interviewing.

Remain consistent in your presentation, narrative, and communication, while showcasing the right attitude. Someone who's good at what they do-at being themself-can back up their claims through embodying the character they take pride in. When being yourself, you don't have to try too hard. Just be the best and most genuine version of you.

ANSWERS TO THE QUESTIONS YOU NEEDN'T ASK

Remember, there are a wide variety of predictable questions you'll likely face in a job interview. Many of them may seem perfectly clear, and other lines of questions may seem confusing. The key to answering all of them is coming prepared and practicing beforehand. Arriving prepared showcases appreciation for the hard work they do and everything their job entails. This is a sign of respect, and that respect should be reciprocated.

When a question they ask you is poorly worded or deliberately confusing, consider it at first a test of your communication skills. Don't answer until you are absolutely sure you are on the same page. Also, anytime you need to, give yourself permission to take a breath, pause, slow down, clarify, while maintaining your confidence and control over your situation.

Don't apologize if something doesn't make sense, or if they are speaking double talk or seemingly trying to confuse you. If it feels like that is what's happening, go the distance to ensure everyone is on the same page. Don't be shy about it. Go to extra lengths to enhance any messy communication.

However, if the person you are interviewing with grows patronizing or impatient with you for requesting clarity, that could be a sign of serious communication breakdowns that exist in their department. Remember the story I shared in the preface to Part Two of this book? That individual's bad behavior was an accurate representation of what working for them would have looked like.

So, if your interviewer's communication skills are lacking, this could clue you into a greater, more systemic explanation for why the position needs to be filled. When that's the case, it begs the question:

✦ Do I really want to work here with them? Is this what I want?

If your answer is no, and you ignore your better judgement and take the job, you won't see the success you are hoping for, and you'll have to live with that choice.

Part Three
Building Upon
Your Professional Worth

Once hired, the real work begins.

Y ou need to ingratiate yourself with every member of the teams you are joining. This is key to building relationships and earning trust. Ask them about themselves, their insights into the company, and for their guidance on how things are done. Ask questions, learn, actively listen, and keep your head down without being a stealth worker. And, when working hard, keep an eye out and seize every opportunity to work smarter.

In order to contribute and showcase everything you offer, you need to always focus on the big picture. But, that big picture can sometimes feel like putting together an unassembled puzzle, with no idea what the image of the completed puzzle looks like. So, to assemble that big picture in your mind, you'll need to absorb all the new information that you can, and piece together that big picture as quickly as you're able.

To do this, always be actively listening. Any chance you have to lean in, study, or learn, seize it. Whenever appropriate, openly eavesdrop. Approach your manager and ask if it's okay if you actively listen. Explain you won't interrupt, that you want to observe, and will volunteer nothing pertaining to what is being discussed. This will help you earn their trust.

Actively listening, every chance you get, will give you stronger insights into operations, and into management's decision-making. Strive to assemble that big picture, and to support the budget and the business's needs. Doing so will help you innovate in ways that are more impactful to the bottom line. The more you learn, the more effectively you'll anticipate need, make informed calculated risks, and rise to any challenge when duty calls.

IT'S A MARATHON, NOT A RACE

Actually, contrary to the age-old adage, a marathon, technically, is a race, albeit a long-distance endurance race. It isn't a sprint or a dash. Some take the lead, while others are not far behind. In a marathon, when you take the lead, you cheer on those trailing close behind you. As for those who are struggling to keep up, someone in the lead might offer a few words of encouragement or wisdom, capitalizing on their strengths and helping them navigate their growth opportunities.

But taking the lead also means being a leader. And being strategic, methodical, motivated, and determined can aid you in rising into a leadership role within your company. This doesn't require assuming a formal leadership position, per se, such as a supervisor or manager. Not at all. It simply means that your work ethic demonstrates your stake in the success of your organization and the overall success of your teams. Ultimately, their success is your success, and vice versa.

View yourself as a future partner, or as a member of the board, and start acting the role passively. Learn the reasoning behind how things are done. Schedule mentor meetings to discuss what you've learned on the job, and ask for insights and directions on how to capitalize on what you've learned, how you can advance your goals, and where the company can take you next. Adopt this systems approach mindset for continually commanding and being rewarded for your professional worth.

In Part Three, we will cover what your leaders ultimately want and desire, how you can increase their budget, how you can make their jobs easier, and ultimately how to get everything you want as soon as they can afford it. And remember, commanding your professional worth is all about making *them* want to give *you* what *you* want.

Chapter 7
Increasing Your Value To The Team

BUILDING RELATIONSHIPS
CROSS-DEPARTMENTALLY

A s we covered in the previous section, when you onboard with any organization, your goals are clear. You have to showcase that you want to learn, to soak up information, and to build relationships.

Consider that, upon starting a new job, you've only been vetted by those who hired you. Therefore, as soon as you walk through those doors for the first time, it's your job to humbly position yourself to be interviewed by all your fellow teammates.

They're going to want to know for themselves whether you'll fit in. So take advantage of this opportunity. Earn the stamp of approval from your teams. Those first impressions matter. By putting in effort into acquiring approval from your colleagues, you'll reinforce the reputation of the recruiter who took a risk on you.

Express curiosity. You're actively learning. Ingratiate them. Lean on others for their insights and perspective. Learn what they do, how they do it, and why they do it. Display respect for what they've accomplished and built. Giving respect earns respect, and thereby trust. Increase your stake in the company, and showcase admiration for their contributions. And as you learn, you need to track everything and document with consistency.

You won't always be the newest member of their team, but while you are, you need to gain support while building your reputation. You also want your team to stand behind you and speak to your merits. Attitude is contagious. So be a bright spot in their day simply through your attitude. Make yourself indispensable to team morale. Enhance the culture and work environment. This will make you invaluable to any organization.

Don't limit your relationships either. It is important to think of yourself as a member of each team in every department. The greater your scope of everyone's role and their stake in the organization's success, the greater your contributions will be. Learn what you can from them about their roles and what they each contribute.

Make friends throughout your organization. Once you've befriended them, take them out to lunch. Then, expand your impact.

KEEP ASKING QUESTIONS

I remember when I was newly promoted into a leadership position. All of my fellow supervisors kept throwing the same coin of advice at me: *Keep Asking Questions.* But knowing which questions to ask wasn't always intuitive. The best way to tackle this problem is simple. Look at asking questions as a passive communication tool. If you have a suggestion for streamlining a bureaucratically bogged-down standard operating procedure, start by asking questions.

Let's say your idea stands to introduce some small incremental improvements that could increase productivity. Instead of approaching your superiors by trying to sell them on your idea, you instead ask questions.

✦ *"I was curious about this system of checks and balances we have. I noticed it feels like there were numerous steps involved, and I've heard our teams grumbling about it on several occasions. I was just curious why these extra steps were implemented."*

This gives your supervisor an incentive to answer an astute question. Once you are filled in, you'll know whether your suggestion would be misplaced. And, if your suggestion still seems like a viable solution, you can then ask:

✦ Has anyone ever tried this before?

Another astute question that suggests leadership potential, merit, and humility. This is opposed to approaching your supervisors with a new great big idea of how to reinvent those standard operating procedures, only to have that obtuse idea shut down. Not a good look.

So, keep asking questions. Never be presumptuous and keep a record of everything you learn. Especially if your suggestion is appreciated, entertained, or implemented. And when that's the case, take note. Consistently asking questions and keeping a photographic image of the big picture in your mind showcases that your work ethic is dependable, reliable, and that you can not only be trusted but be counted on.

EVERY ASPECT OF EVERYTHING YOU DO

As you learn, how you keep track of everything is up to you. Only you can determine the best systems approach for cataloguing and tracking everything you're responsible for. For example, let's say one day you find yourself in an especially complicated situation that requires you to re-prioritize your current workload. Suddenly, you are multitasking and have to keep track of several half-fulfilled responsibilities which you now need to hit pause on. To ensure you don't drop the ball on any one of them, you track it all in the notebook you keep in your back pocket. When it's time to resume those tasks, it's all in there, and you have forgotten nothing and haven't dropped a single ball.

However, your notebook contains much more than just that. You've also noted advice you offered your peers, the coaching you delivered, how you stepped up and volunteered when someone was needed to go the extra mile, or when volunteering meant stepping outside of your comfort zone. Every single thing you do for the organization and for your teams and individual teammates, you've continually notated in your notebook. This way, you have a full report of all of your accomplishments and the progress you've made.

The more you track your commitments, failures, accomplishments, and your contributions to the team's achievements, the more successfully you can perform a self-evaluation. And, meeting with your manager or mentor monthly, while reporting on what you've documented and what you've learned from your setbacks and mistakes–and what you've contributed to the organization's success–will offer documented proof of your value.

You are building your professional profile and image by reporting on every detail that commands your professional worth. Nothing is open to interpretation or up for debate. If anyone took credit for your accomplishments, this also gives you a clear opportunity to reclaim it.

This is the path of a samurai. Living with honor and making your documented progress and victories known and quantifiable. Your goal is to showcase your time management skills and your project management skills by reaching each of those attainable milestones and career goals you set for yourself, in the measured timeframes by which you aimed to achieve them.

Remember, every organization would prefer to profit off of stealth workers without having to reward them for their contributions. Not having to share their profits means more for those at the top. It's your duty to advocate for yourself. You are your own advocate, and you are the only person you can count on. And this book provides the systems method you need. Every day you'll continue to build upon the databank that measures your professional worth. You'll walk the walk. You'll talk the talk. You'll maintain control over your trajectory. And, as you continue to rise up, you'll continue to embody your worth for all to see.

DEVELOPING & DEFINING YOUR SYSTEMS & PROCESSES

Once it's clear how your team and workplace operate, you can focus on making a greater impact. This requires not only developing systems and processes, but also being able to clearly communicate them to others. This can sometimes prove challenging. However, the more you meditate on defining your abstract approach to solving problems, the better you'll be at articulating them. And the more effective you are at articulating your approach to your work, the more resourceful you'll be at whipping up logical and effective systems and processes when no others are in place.

When difficult situations arise that require outside of the box thinking, you'll be better equipped to handle those high-stakes situations on the fly, with fail-safes planned in. Lastly, on this point, you will be able to more effectively define your professional worth by articulating in layman's terms your integral value to the organization as their *clutch player.*

INTEGRAL TO THE TEAM

After your first 90-day trial period, you're fully integrated into your team. You'll have proven yourself and paid your dues. You'll understand how things work and why they're run the way they are. As the adage goes, you have to know the rules before you break them. The greater your insight into how things work, and what goes into everyone else's job, the more effective you'll be at making their jobs easier.

This starts with being reliably professional, uplifting, and positive, which requires maintaining absolute control of every aspect of your life. The more in control you feel, the more confident you will seem. So start by taking measures to lower your controllable daily stress while enhancing your work-life balance.

WORK LIFE BALANCE

When your personal life and work-life are off balance, work-stress affects your personal life, and your personal-stress impacts your work. On either spectrum, this isn't a good look. It compromises the perception of your professional worth. There's only one way to manage stress. To pre-emptively eliminate every controllable stress factor you can.

In Chapter Two, we described what a morning looked like for someone who has no time management or organizational skills, which directly impacted their work-life balance. Let's dive deeper into those two scenarios that individual faced, on a daily basis. Better yet, to take it a step farther, I want you to walk around in their shoes.

In the first scenario, we'll exemplify what having an imbalance between your work and home looks like. In the second scenario, we'll portray success. Starting with *scenario one*, let's say you had a terrible day at work. You simply couldn't wait to get home to decompress with a glass of wine and a comforting meal. You went to bed, wasting half the night obsessing over your stress. You finally fell asleep obsessing about the dread of what the next work day will bring.

Morning comes, and when the alarm goes off, you hit snooze too many times. You eventually rise up and are moving slowly. By the time you've had your coffee, you look at the clock. You're running late, and cortisol levels rise. Springing into gear, you leap into the shower, and that soothing, nice hot shower causes you to slow down again. Upon exiting the shower, you panic when you realize how much more time has passed. So, now you're racing again.

You don't have time to pack a lunch. So much for eating at your desk. And now you're stressed about spending money by eating out yet again. Just as you're about to leave, you spot the note you left for yourself. You still haven't disputed that bill, or cancelled that personal engagement, or rescheduled that doctor's appointment. When you came home last night, you intentionally put it off. Now, your cortisol levels are on the rise again.

You hurry out the door and jump in your car. To arrive at work on time, you'll need to speed and disregard stop signs and lights. Then you notice a stain on your shirt because you forgot to do laundry. Then you notice the gas light is on and you need to fill your gas tank. Panic sinks in. When it's all said and done, you're only five minutes late for work and nobody seems to notice. But your cortisol levels are through the roof. *And,* your stress shows at work anytime something doesn't go according to plan. Everyone notices your stress, and your negativity infects workplace morale. Pretty soon everyone is in a bad mood.

Throughout the day, anytime you have a micro break, you're on the phone trying to reschedule that doctor's appointment, or to dispute that bill, all while you are on the clock. In *scenario one,* you brought home the stresses of your workday, which negatively impacted your personal life. Then, how disorganized your personal life was impacted your attitude and your performance at work, eroding workplace morale. At the end of the day, you barely met expectations. Most of that situation was completely within your control. Not just your attitude, but your planning and time management.

Now let's look at *scenario two.* After having a great day, you leave work. Earlier on, your team ran into some obstacles, and a coworker let their stress get a hold of them. But you're aware that they are going through some personal problems, and you are empathetic. So, you led by example, helped calm the situation, and set the pace for the work that needed to be done. All goals were achieved, and the day was saved. You didn't take sole credit, but accredited the team for the group's success. Yet, your impact was noticed, and you've documented it.

As you head home, you take a little extra time to cap off your gas tank. In practice, you do this every day, and your tank never runs on empty. Always running your car on an empty gas tank is harder on the fuel systems, the engine, and increases maintenance costs. Keeping the tank full ensures you never have to fill it in the morning. Yesterday, you took care of that bill that you disputed, you changed that appointment, as well as addressed all of your other personal obligations that needed addressing.

Last Sunday, you spent the day cooking and freezing your meals for the rest of the week. You almost always have a prepared lunch to bring with you to work, and your dinner is ready and waiting to be reheated when you get home. Your laundry was also addressed, folded or hung, and you planned out your outfits for the week. You identify idle moments to cross more things off of your list by multitasking. Such as how, on your drive home, you typically make any calls you need to make- taking care of things that fall in the in-between personal and professional spheres.

Scenario two has you arriving home stress-free, and you spend the evening any way you like. You go for a run, hike, bike ride, hit the gym, or do pilates or yoga.

You enjoy your glass of wine and you are grateful and happy for the delicious meal that was waiting for you.

You get ready for bed and read some engaging industry-related content. You learn everything you can, furthering your knowledge and skills in your field of expertise. Then you turn off the light. You take your supplements which aid your sleep and have a restful and worry-free rejuvenating night. You wake up well-rested. Your coffee is already awaiting you. You read the news and generate some fun water cooler talk. You take a stress-free shower, climb into the clothes that are washed and pressed. Your ride to work is peaceful. You arrive early, have another cup of coffee, and warmly greet and check in with everyone you work with before you start your day.

Scenario one compromises your professional worth and detrimentally impacts your quality of life. Whereas *scenario two* increases both your quality of life and increases your professional worth, and is exemplary of a strong work-life balance.

The most amazing thing about this system's approach mindset is its simplicity. Anyone can do it. It doesn't take practice. It just takes forming the right habits, which in turn build discipline. But I look at it this way. It's the discipline of guaranteeing more time for the things you want—your personal interests, hobbies, and everything that makes you more interesting. It's all about prioritizing your quality of life. Even more so, it secures your power over you.

BURNOUT VERSUS JOB SATISFACTION

Your work-life balance will directly impact your propensity to burnout on the job, or reinforce how rewarding and fulfilling your career is. So many of *scenario one's* stresses were avoidable. *Scenario one* showcased someone who took no control of their life and suffered the consequences. They also took no ownership and little responsibility. Whereas *scenario two* is a perfect example of practicing successful time management skills, simply by scheduling in time to manage competing priorities-your personal life and your professional life-which creates more time for being the best version of yourself.

Consider it as going the extra mile for yourself. This is the big picture of your success. Taking control of your controllable stress factors empowers you. It makes you more confident and offers more control over your life. Allocating time for recharging ensures you're prepared for the day ahead. You've anticipated and planned for contingencies, and arrive at work early. If traffic slowed because of an accident, and you called work to forewarn of a slight chance of being late–a rare occurrence, your thoughtfulness would be valued, highlighting your excellent attendance without appearing sycophantic.

Most importantly, it showcases being mindful of the big picture. The less stress you have, the greater your job satisfaction will be. Your attitude impacts the morale of your team, and whether people enjoy being around you. It also helps you strengthen your relationships with your coworkers, both inside and outside of work. All of these amount to you being an irreplaceable member of the team, which increases your power in the workplace. In *scenario two*, the grass is never greener on the other side; rather, it's always the greenest where you're standing.

RESOURCEFULNESS

When you have a high stress threshold, you can lead by example and are capable of thinking quickly on your feet when the need arises. The more your brain is recharged and the greater your work-life balance is, the more creative you'll be in finding solutions to problems. Being in the practice of documenting everything sharpens your attention to detail. The more you observe, the more you will notice. When you have a high stress threshold, you can lead by example and are capable of thinking quickly on your feet when the need arises.

Anytime you can think outside-of-the-box or step outside of your comfort zone, you are indispensable to the team. This includes being resourceful and finding solutions even when you don't have everything you need to solve a problem. These are what make you a leader. Your attitude informs your perspective and sets a standard for how others perceive you. The more positive things the members of your team have to say about you, the better.

Reading about what is happening in the industry will build your reputation. You'll be seen by your teammates and peers as a resource of valuable information. The more informed you are, with your finger on the pulse and your ear to the ground, the more effective you'll be at anticipating trends or overcoming obstacles which can also easily be averted. You should never limit this to industry news either. Stay up to date on your organization's news and blog. This will help you serve as a better representative, and as the voice of their brand.

There's nothing worse than your employer overhearing a client asking you a question you can't answer. This forces your employer to step in. On the other hand, there's nothing better than when a customer asks your boss a question about your industry and they don't know the answer, and you politely step in and ask if it's alright for you to answer the question. What that communicates to both your boss and your customer is that they hired the right person for the job.

KAIZEN TO INNOVATION

It's important to always measure your contributions to your team and the workplace. Documenting isn't enough. In fact, once a week in your spare time, or during micro-breaks, you need to transfer what you've documented to your database–your contributions to the team and to your organization–anything and everything that falls outside of meeting expectations.

For example, merely arriving on time or early to work is expected. Yet, de-escalating workplace conflicts, steering the team morale in the right direction, and supporting your leader's vision exceeds expectations. Making incremental improvements or suggestions (kaizen) or earth-shattering improvements that yielded instant gains (innovation) goes above and beyond. Keep your weekly report up to date, and separate them by month.

What you need to convey, when contextualizing your narrative, is how your work standard is above and beyond, and how you are always trying to best your personal best, while pacing yourself on the marathon of your professional self-improvement.

It showcases that you have a bird's-eye view of the big picture of your career, and how your career fits into their organization. It reveals that you are relied upon for your professional knowledge and acumen, and that you walk the walk and talk the talk.

You know your worth and what the organization values you for. You act in the department's best interest. And you're a stakeholder in the success of every individual you work with. And you always ensure that credit is given where credit is due. You're aware of other employees' needs and make sure their merits are rewarded as well. You share the spotlight when appropriate. And, you guarantee their trust in you will always be rewarded.

RISK-TAKER OR RISK AVERSE?

Someone who is a compulsive risk-taker gets off on the rush of playing with power. And, in a casino environment, status symbols of power are commonly cash winnings, and the daring to risk it all. A big roller or a baller are common words used to glorify this. Pejoratives are dice fiend, slot junkie, or degenerate.

There are also those who are risk-averse. Typically, these individuals stick to performing the ins and outs of their job, according to their job description, and rarely deviate. When a crisis arises at work, they freeze up. They prefer to play it safe and wait around for someone with more authority to make that time-sensitive decision. Both the compulsive risk-taker and the person who plays it safe are liabilities.

Also, there are those who can't identify risk when they see it. For example, you should never bite off more than you can chew. Doing so will only undermine your time management skills, generate stress while over-extending yourself, all while building a reputation for over-promising and under-delivering. This is similar to making leadership decisions that fall outside of your authority, skill, or scope.

As you pursue your career goals, you'll find yourself competing for the opportunity to contribute and rise up. And, every time you vie for a developmental opportunity, you need to identify the risks involved, and take every measure to shore up your success.

A person who always asks questions, who understands the types of risks those in positions of authority would likely make, and takes a well-informed calculated risk in a high-pressure situation that requires swift action is someone who can make a well-informed, calculated risk. When they play their hand, they have a full house, and there's little risk in them taking their own bets. They are an asset.

Such an individual also learns from their mistakes, increasing their track record for success. They actively listen so they can anticipate need, are trusted to lead when no other leaders are available. It positions them as a stakeholder who is invested in driving the vision of their organization forward. They increase their professional worth simply by protecting the assets of the organization.

WHAT ARE YOU WORTH TO YOUR TEAMS?

Maintain a sharp eye on your self-awareness, and what your peers value you for. Then document it. Be mindful of your psychological impact. You want everything you offer to speak for itself, all while being your strongest advocate.

Remember, consistency is everything. Being reliable in your performance standard means never sliding backwards. Perception is reality. If you experience a setback. Own it and actionably display growth. When you do that, that mistake won't happen again. Keep setting the pace, leading by example, boosting morale, pacing yourself, and taking on only as much as you can manage. This is how you command the respect of your teams while increasing your worth to the organization.

Chapter 8
Tying Your Value
To Their Bottom Line

G etting hired at a desirable rate is a challenge
most people face. It's even harder to be
rewarded for your efforts when performance
reviews come around. In fact, too many feel like they're
at the mercy of their superior's generosity. And, too
often, they surrender, settling into a job they don't even
like, while gratefully accepting any minor pay increase
at all.

In these final two chapters, we'll break down how to
ensure you're rewarded according to your professional

worth. I'll offer advice on how to keep pay raise negotiations open, and how to ensure you leave nothing on the table, nor miss an opportunity to rise up and increase your standing, your worth, and your potential.

ESTABLISHING YOUR EXPECTATIONS

There are many games and dirty tricks to expect when performance reviews come around. For example, when you're successful at negotiating a higher pay rate when hired, your managers might later surprise you by claiming you don't qualify for a raise on your first performance review, since they brought you in at a higher rate. A more likely explanation is that they failed to meet their goals, and their budget fell short or was mismanaged, and now they are trying to cut corners anywhere they can.

This, from a business perspective, is simply an example of poor leadership. Rhetorically speaking, how is it fair for them to pay you less for your performance indicators when theirs fell short? Having asked that question sparks an even bigger rhetorical question–isn't it a red flag that they're not adhering to their values, and that they are not truly transparent? This then begs an even bigger question: was this actually a good career move after all?

This is why it's important to negotiate salary–and pay increase percentage–before deciding if you'll accept their offer of employment. Negotiating a reasonable pay increase percentage upon meeting your objectives by your first performance review–unless that review is within a couple of months of getting hired—is just as important as negotiating your development goals and how often you'll have development meetings.

The cleanest dirty trick they might employ is where they guise not being able to meet your expectations with '*transparency*,' and claim they fell short of their targets. Hypothetically, let's say you negotiated—contingent on your acceptance of their offer of employment—that if you met your goals, you'd be rewarded for your projected value in the industry according to your professional growth. They agree to your terms—saying anything they need to get you to come onboard. Then, later, they claim they fell short of their targets and unexpectedly would not be able to give you, or anyone else, a raise. That's a breach of contract, and something they could have clearly foreseen long in advance before making such false promises.

This underlines the importance of documenting everything you learn about the inner workings of the business. Never be ignorant of their bottom line. You see, too often, those in leadership positions rely on your ignorance in order to hold you back. They can then blame factors that are beyond your understanding for not paying you more. Ideally, they'll want to distribute their payroll budget in a manner in which they get paid more of that budget while you get paid less. The hungrier you are, the more power they have. They can then get you to work harder without compensating you fairly. This is the epitome of a carrot and stick career progression. They set the terms, dictate, and compromise your professional worth, rendering you powerless.

And, if your superiors are holding you to a higher standard then they need to reward you for that standard; otherwise, you'll find yourself stuck in that carrot and stick career progression. And, the ultimate goal of a carrot and stick career progression is to squeeze you for all your potential until you're burned out. Once you're completely burned out, they'll end your employment and replace you with someone new, in a similar pay grade, who'll likely fall for their same dirty tricks. This is more common than you think and paints a bleak big picture.

This is why you want to ensure replacing you would cost more than convincing you to stay on. By working smarter, leading by example, and setting the pace, you performed stronger than any single member of the team, and the team benefits from having you as a member. If your team looks forward to working with you, then you are integral to morale. Yet, even then, they may try to avoid giving you a significant raise unless they are convinced they may lose you as an employee.

As we previously covered, vacancies increase the workload for the rest of the team and negatively impact morale. Recruiting impacts payroll and stretches the budget. Even if they were to hire one person to replace someone who performed the job of three people, productivity has still dropped off. And, when the team burns out on the job, the entire brand suffers.

Remember, every decision you make takes you somewhere. So maintain a clear view of what lies ahead before blindly marching on. Try not to make any wrong turns and be mindful not to take someone else's poor directions. Don't change course or stray off your path. Stay true to your trajectory.

ADVOCATE FOR YOURSELF

If you find your career stalling, you'll want to assert yourself. Schedule time with your manager to discuss your career progression. Detail the opportunities you'd like to seize next. Command the time to advertise your accomplishments–what you've learned, where you've improved and shown progress, and the opportunities you've identified which could further the goals of the organization. This circumvents any stalling tactics, and sets a precedent for what you are worth, week by week, month after month.

It also establishes clear expectations. You're calling attention to your contributions, and why they should be rewarded, without having to directly say so. By making it clear you are career driven and determined to rise further up within specified timelines, they can't get away with paying less than you are worth. Concerning performance reviews, a ninja will almost always receive a lousy raise and poor scores. This is commonly attributed to simply trusting that their superiors will do the right thing. But advocating for your professional worth is never a simple matter. You need to claim and call attention to your victories. This is integral to building your reputation. So, be a samurai, and not a ninja.

I'll never forget the performance review I received where my scores were all labeled as barely meeting expectations. I was shocked and spent the next forty minutes contesting those scores with my boss. I'd spent the last six months putting my all in, and my accomplishments were far above and beyond what my fellow supervisors were putting in.

That's when my boss said,

"We knew stuff was getting done, but no one took credit for it. I didn't know it was you. If what you're saying is true, that means you're a stealth worker. When we don't know what you were doing, it just seemed like you're cruising along, barely meeting expectations. Well, it's too late now. Reviews are done, and unfortunately at this point I can't increase your pay rate any further. Better luck next time. Just make your presence known and keep up the good work."

I was furious and frustrated. Then, when I reflected on all the previous advice I was given, I realized that advice was nothing more than a carrot dangling on a string from a stick. Empty advice suspended from a false promise. So, I took matters into my own hands.

I no longer relied on the generosity or kindness of my peers. I started documenting everything. Not only what I was accomplishing, but the state of the morale of our teams, what impacted morale, and what my fellow supervisors were doing—especially when it concerned the company's assets. I then took the calculated risk of deciding which matters to address and improve on my own and only brought those of a more serious matter to the attention of my boss. He didn't need to know everything that was going on. All he needed to know was that I took care of it and had everything under control. I made his job easier so he could focus on bigger picture concerns.

I basically built a case to undermine every excuse they used to not reward me for my efforts. Then, I made sure I had half an hour a month to bend the ear of my boss. A year later, I asked if we still needed to have these monthly meetings, and he said, *"No. That won't be necessary. I know what you're contributing."*

At that point, I requested meetings only as needed— which sometimes were every month, and other times were twice a week. And, if you'll remember from earlier in the book, when I left the company, my boss later told me that he wished I never quit, and that things have never been the same since I left. That informed me that it wasn't until I left that he truly understood the impact I was making, including how much easier his job was as a result of my contributions.

By scheduling a closed-door meeting with a decision-making manager, you'll be advocating for yourself and making your impact known. However, if you meet with a supervisor who you work closely with, who already has a lot on their plate, and they neglect to report the progress and content of your meetings to the manager who decides who gets a raise, you're back to square one.

Also, don't think of it as sycophantic. You are initiating transparent engagement and taking command of your professional worth. You are being a leader of your own destiny, tapping into your own potential, and acting as a samurai who's making your loyalty and value known. Having your teammates and peers cheer you on is not reward enough. You are owed your due.

Now, once you have your momentum going, always be prepared for career contingencies. Such as making progress with a mentor or manager that you've recruited to your cause, who then ends up transferring, quitting, or advancing into a different position. When this happens, you may find yourself starting all over with a new boss. Remember, attitude is everything. Nothing is forever, and now you're practiced.

If you are having trouble getting the attention of the new manager, ask to meet with them. If they won't make the time, meet with your old boss and request advice on how to work with, and help, your new boss. You're just trying to support the organization during a period of transition while making everyone's job easier.

NO NEWS IS BAD NEWS

Be proactive. Take advantage of every opportunity to request feedback from your peers and superiors alike. It showcases humility and drive while building upon your EQ and your reputation. Determine what you can do better. And try to take the good with the bad, without fishing for compliments.

Be open, and never immediately respond to any feedback you are given. Always be non-defensive. Also, ask them if they are open to you asking more questions later as you think of them. Whatever the feedback, whether fair, unwarranted, misplaced, or poorly phrased, there's always something to learn.

When the messaging of the feedback you receive feels harsh, aggressive, frustrated, unfair, or poorly communicated, never debate or make excuses or grow defensive. Be calm and confident. Ask clarifying questions and be the stronger communicator.

Thank them for their input and tell them you will take some time to process and consider what they've said. This will also disarm any aggression the person delivering the feedback may have had in their delivery. It gives space and time to let their comments breathe, and if their criticisms were unnecessarily harsh, they may end up apologizing for them later and give you a revised version of the feedback they offered.

Dig deeper and determine what went wrong, whether it was interpersonal relations, communication problems, or if real improvement needs to be seen. Seek additional input, especially when you feel you are no closer to the answers you're seeking.

This will help you paint a more accurate self-evaluation for when you deliver your monthly self-performance review. The more you do this, the stronger your sense of self-awareness will be.

HOW TO RISE UP
WHILE PRESERVING YOUR REPUTATION

You'll want to always seek out feedback, to grow and improve at every opportunity, to keep your record clean, all while supporting your teams. Identify your most trusted allies and never allow yourself to be undermined by competitors in the workplace. The entire aim is to get along with everyone, while avoiding engaging in gossip and back-talking, and keeping anything management shares with you to yourself, unless they advise you to distribute that information. Adhere strictly to their code of ethics and conduct, and always protect the integrity and reputation of the organization.

Be open and transparent in all of your conduct. Always think three moves ahead. Most importantly, be in the habit of documenting everything–questions, ideas, KPIs, accomplishments, setbacks, concerning conduct and inappropriate conversations, or anything you deem noteworthy.

Similar to developing your organizational skills and time management skills, this all boils down to habit and operating in a certain way. If it seems tedious, it hasn't become a habit yet. But this is the job description of working towards your own goals, furthering your career, and increasing your professional worth.

You need to go beyond documenting your accomplishments, beyond delivering self-performance evaluations, and beyond requesting realistic input from your superiors. You also need to pay keen attention to the levels at which your peers are delivering compared to yours, including your superiors. Showcase how you are promoting their growth, how you *manage up*, all while setting the pace. In short, you're leading by example and showcasing your own leadership potential while helping their bottom line.

Once you've developed these professional habits, you'll be in a much stronger position. It all boils down to valuing yourself, and securing your power, while ensuring no one can take it from you, nor allowing anyone to convince you that you are less than you have proven yourself to be, in tangible and substantiated terms.

This is no different from the organization mapping out their fiscal goals and quarterly planning. You are running your career like a successful business. So set your mind on what you want, whether it is that overseas position in Dublin, that corner office, or becoming a member of the board. It is up to you what milestone comes next, and what comes after that.

INCREASING YOUR STAKE

We've already discussed continually asking questions. But once you feel you've learned the ropes and have a clear lay of the land, it's time to ramp up the questions you ask. To really shape others' perception of your worth, you'll want to express interest in all the bigger inner workings of the organization. You want to demonstrate that you truly are a stakeholder in their success. This isn't difficult to do. In fact, it is quite passive. It's about asking the right questions in a manner that aligns with your nature.

For example, understanding the cross-functionality of the organization, in depth, expands your lens. In fact, just being in the know increases your worth. The more you know, the stronger your negotiating power will be. And the more interest you show as you continue to learn, the more supportive you can be in making your superiors' jobs easier. This will help you accomplish your goals and to gain the incentives you are vying for, all by aligning your motivators with theirs. In layman's terms, you are learning and identifying the perfect indisputable angle to take for rising up and getting what you want.

But asking questions and pursuing lines of inquiry pertaining to the inner workings of the business is a balancing act. You first have to establish yourself as a coordinated team player. Be a clutch player, positioning yourself to be relied upon, always ready to rise up and get it done. And the more balanced you are, the more effective you'll be.

You'll effortlessly exceed expectations at no cost to you. You'll always be working smarter rather than harder. This includes having a high EQ, exceptional communication skills, and being able to delegate without being bossy or overstepping your bounds.

Delegation requires more than explaining *what* needs to be done. It also requires explaining *why* it needs to be done. All of this must be expertly communicated where the team can be trusted to self-manage with the information and instructions they were provided.

Everyone is a stakeholder in the group effort, in the organization's success, and their assembled outcomes. Every work assignment is a piece of that puzzle. When the puzzle is put together, it assembles the complete big picture. So, clarify expectations. Specify deadlines and make the impact of the work clear.

Now, you've likely heard the adage;

> ### *If you want something done right, you have to do it yourself.*

This should be rephrased as;

> *If you have too much difficulty explaining how to do the job right, expectations will be unclear and outcomes will be missed. If you prefer to give up on explaining it, it's because you lack the communication skills to do so, and maybe then it's just easier to do it yourself.*

Now what about when you're on the receiving end of poor delegation? Let's consider a scenario where you followed their instructions precisely, only to discover that it was the instructions themselves that were flawed. Who is to blame? That entirely depends on whether the leader who communicated poorly will take responsibility, or use you as a scapegoat for their mistakes.

To ensure you never take the blame for not doing a job right when your instructions and expectations were unclear, you need to repeat their instructions back to them, write them down, and make certain the message they intend to send is the message indeed being received. And, you need to ask the right questions.

✦ How does this work fit into the big picture?

✦ How does it relate to the work you've assigned to other members of the team?

✦ What are the stakes involved?

✦ What is the impact of my contribution?

✦ Is there anything else I can do to contribute?

✦ What, when, how, why, where, and who?

Consistently showcase you are always trying to outperform your personal best by working smarter rather than harder, and always follow up and ask how you could have done better.

✦ What were the results of the team's efforts?

✦ Did we, as a group, hit all our targets?

✦ What else could I have done to support the team effort?

WHAT YOU WANT BENEFITS THE ORGANIZATION

For example, let's say you want to take two days off next week. Before requesting those days off, keep an eye out for opportunities. Like how, two days later that week, the department is short-staffed by one person. The days you want off are low-impact days, and the days the team is short-staffed are high-impact days.

So instead, you tell your employer you looked at your schedule, and realized if you switched days off for work this week, it would help the business on those days that the department was short-staffed. You're doing it for the business, and you've motivated them to give you what you want. There must always be an alignment. Advocate for what you want by detailing how it benefits the organization.

You want them to invest in your career and to advance your professional worth. So, to understand their big picture goals, learn their vision for the next quarter, and the quarter after that, all the way forward into the next five years. In other words, how does their vision and forecasted business plan align with your five-year career plan? What primary goals are they aiming to accomplish? What is the messaging behind those goals?

Reach across the aisle as well and engage with key players in other departments. Learn about the key functions of their roles. The more informed you are about how the business works, the stronger your positioning will be when advocating for your professional worth. Building relationships across departments also opens up more avenues for rising up within the organization.

Also, keeping up to date with the organization's news, media attention, YouTube presence, and reports makes you a trusted resource and offers you opportunities to open new dialogue as a stakeholder in their success.

When it comes to acquiring broader insight and digging into deeper subject material, you might ask to sit down with your manager to discuss these broader topics, as well as discussing the future of your career with the company. Accommodate their schedule and even suggest you could come in early to make that meeting easier on them. Be assertive and be boundaried. Keep it professional.

When you align your goals with the organization, you're taking charge of your own career. Support your teams, anticipate need, understand the business, and support the organization's vision. Doing so will make you more valuable while increasing your power.

BUILDING & PROTECTING YOUR REPUTATION

Building a reputation as a stakeholder or future partner requires an operational understanding of the business. Remain in the dark, and you won't have the vaguest idea of how much they can afford to pay you.

Once you understand how the business works, you'll also have a better concept of what you can do to help them grow and how to make the biggest positive impacts on their bottom line, which increases your indispensable worth. The more you learn, the more you'll be able to increase your stake in the organization. You'll constantly look out for your mutual interests while further building upon your reputation.

A negative side effect here is the unwelcome competition you might attract. And even though your approach is passively assertive, some might perceive you as a threat. Especially if your rate of ascension outpaces theirs. When this is the case, observe any tensions that arise and document them objectively. You don't want to look like you're building a case against them. You just want to create a paper trail, leaving little to speculation or recollection. And if the unfortunate should happen, and you face more aggressive threats, you'll need to handle those swiftly with a heightened level of emotional intelligence and situational leadership.

Let's examine a worse-case example:

Harassment and intimidation—Every situation will be unique. Bringing up incidents of sexual harassment and intimidation carries risk. Raising an alarm can damage your reputation as a result of systematic bias. It can also invite judgement and bring out the worst in people.

Keeping quiet can be even more damaging and generate terrible stress. Silence can invite even more harassment and create a hostile work environment from which there seems no escape. Both of these are damaging to your career and reputation. What is important here is how to achieve your goals at zero cost to you. What does that look like? Making the person responsible for the harassment and intimidation accountable for their actions. Justice. Using the rules of the game to your advantage and winning.

It's worth mentioning that I have endured sexual harassment in the workplace, from both men and women alike. While anyone can fall victim to sexual harassment, I need to acknowledge the fact that I in no way claim to compare my experience to what women endure on a far more frequent basis. My only intention is to share my experience and what I learned from my mistakes.

Regarding my experiences, these individuals both held positions of power, each in their own way. We'll start with the man. He was a cop who worked as our security on certain days of the week. His overtures were aggressive, constant, and sometimes intimidating. This experience was new to me, and I am an ally of the LGBTQ+ community, and had no interest in promoting any stereotypes or tropes or triggering homophobia. Yet, as an aggressive police officer, he had power, and the last thing I wanted to do was have his aggressive and intimidating behavior ramp up. So, I made a poor decision; I remained silent. And this intimidation continued, at work, at work parties, and every passive manner I took to curb his overtures all failed or sent the wrong signal. Finally, it stopped when I transferred to another location.

The other occasion was with a woman, and her motives weren't entirely clear. She was the niece of the regional manager and was a fellow supervisor who frequently used questionable tactics to promote her interests. One day, when she believed we were alone, she stepped closer and leeringly looked me up and down. The words she said next were clearly meant as a sexual innuendo. It was extremely out of character. I don't know if she miscalculated my loyalty to my wife or if she was setting a trap. In fact, my mind doesn't work this way, so I cannot entertain what she was thinking. But, luckily she didn't notice my co-worker who was around the corner and heard and witnessed the entire thing. Upon her departure, my coworker's wild eyes validated my shock.

So, with some room for improvement as to how I could have addressed it, I documented the incident, addressed it with my manager, and took no action other than that. I just wanted, this time, to make sure the incident was never repeated. However, the regional manager got word of it, and that did nothing to improve my situation. That, along with other factors, drew my career with that company to a close.

Having offered all this, I am still a man, and my experiences never led to an actual physical assault, and it never got to the point where I felt my life was at risk. And, no matter how either scenario could have potentially played out, my circumstances will never be comparable to that of a woman. So, again, the advice I offer is solely from my perspective and experience, and with an understanding of this power differential, and how it can perpetually impact one's career.

So, moving forward, let's hypothetically say you are a supervisor, and have earned the favor of your employer. You are the rising star. And, a fellow supervisor envies your position. So, in a calculated move, when the two of you are alone, that competing supervisor employs a sickening tactic designed to undermine your credibility. This tactic relies on you to sabotage yourself, while creating the perception that you may be a liability for the organization.

What was their plan? To strategically intimidate you in the form of sexual harassment, in a manner which seems uncharacteristic even for them. They choose their words cleverly, so if you were to relay them second-hand, they would seem open to interpretation. Now, it's your word against theirs.

Their plan relies on you reporting the incident. Doing so will burden administration, and result in company revenue losses. They also want you to be visibly agitated, weakened and vulnerable, a victim, and someone who responds emotionally rather than professionally. They want you to seem unstable, while they calmly maintain their innocence and claim it was a misunderstanding.

Should you inform your manager of what's happened? Absolutely. But how you address the situation is important. You need to play their game against them.

Remember, a ninja is a saboteur, and if you handle this incorrectly, you will sabotage your own career. View this from a samurai's perspective. A samurai has a mission and follows a code. When they strike, they do so without emotion, only honor. And they strike with surgical precision. If emotion enters the equation, they sheath their sword and wait until they are centered once more.

When someone attacks a samurai, they deflect the attack in such a way that delivers that blow back upon the attacker. So, when someone attacks you, deflect their aggressive maneuver. Victory is achieved when they've only succeeded in hurting themself.

In the aforementioned scenario, you ask your boss if you can have a moment in private. You describe the escalating tension with your fellow supervisor that you have studied and observed, and documented for some time.

At first, you took unbiased notes pertaining to their performance. But then this incident occurred, and you found it so concerning it was worth addressing with your superior. You then objectively describe how the events unfolded, and the various ways his actions and choice of words could be interpreted. You theorize he was either attempting to intimidate and harass, or he was entirely unaware of how his actions could be perceived by others, either of which poses a serious liability for the business. You express how this seemed uncharacteristic of them, yet their emotional output has been consistently erratic as of late.

You speculate that if he was ill-intentioned, he's potentially demonstrated such behavior before, and may repeat it again. By highlighting this, you detail the risks he presents, even if this situation was a one-off. If lacking self-awareness, who knows how others might perceive and interpret his actions? Giving him the benefit of the doubt, this lack of self-awareness presents a serious growth opportunity. He's a liability, and his progress might need to be tracked.

You want to make it clear you aren't necessarily making a formal complaint, but wanted to address this problem before his actions repeat and he creates a real PR nightmare for the organization. If that were to happen, it would bog down human resources, cost the company in legal fees, result in the expense of sensitivity training, and lost productivity. No matter how you look at it, ultimately it impacts the bottom line. You lastly inform your manager that you have documented the entire incident and have it stored in a secure, password-protected file, and would be happy to forward them a copy of the report if they would like the paper trail.

This unemotional approach objectively looks out for the best interests of the organization. It also protects you from further intimidation. If that supervisor takes it further, you have informed management and created a paper trail. You've made the incident known, showcasing yourself as an asset and them as a liability. When you've already built a strong reputation for yourself, you can trust that your word and credibility carry weight.

Ultimately, every situation is unique. There will always be those who will try to find some weakness they can exploit. So when it comes to protecting yourself and your interests and feeling safe, respond without emotion and do whatever you feel is strategically right for you. If you need it, find trustworthy support and do everything you can to preserve your work-life balance and your reputation.

WHERE YOUR IMPACT CAN TAKE THEM NEXT

The goal is to make evident your investment potential. Such as traveling for work, representing the organization at a conference or event, fundraising, and handling their PR. The more you have to offer, the more they have to gain. You also want to establish realistic expectations of what they can and will accommodate pertaining to your pay, incentives, training, and increased stake in the organization's success.

You want to go above and beyond being a representative for their organization. This is how you can acquire access to their full big picture, and the best path forward for maximizing your professional worth.

WHAT DO THEY HAVE TO WORK WITH?

By now, your contributions to the workplace culture are known and indispensable. You have increased your professional worth. Your superiors know your efforts must be rewarded.

But without knowing what they can afford to pay you, how can you know what to ask for? If you've followed the advice in this book, you've been expanding your understanding of the business. You're taking notes, actively listening, asking questions, and are a trusted resource of information.

But you are now at the crossroads. Will you be absorbed into their system and embody their business—and does their business embody success—or will you make their systems work for you while simultaneously supporting yourself and them?

To answer these questions, you need to keep tabs on their allocated budgets. How much is allotted to each department and each project, from payroll, to marketing, to IT, to rent? How much of the organization's profits or fundraising are spoken for? What are the KPIs and fiscal goals that you might impact? How can you help?

If you have your finger on the pulse of the industry, what information or innovative suggestions would be useful to improving the bottom line, like bringing in a new CRM (customer relationship management system), or a new human resource management system to help cut costs and streamline systems and departmental efficiency?

The stronger your understanding of their budget, fiscal goals, allocated funds, the victories, and setbacks they're facing–and anywhere there is room to make a positive impact–the greater your positioning will be. When you have a bigger picture of what they can actually afford to pay you–according to your ever-increasing worth–the more negotiating power you have. If their payroll budget is stretched, and you're bringing in new accounts and generating more business, then you could maybe even try negotiating a commission.

HOW TO NOT TAKE *NO* FOR AN ANSWER

So, you've planned out your milestones and have come to an arrangement with your employer on how to meet those goals and progress your career. You are hyper-aware of the trappings of a carrot and stick career progression. In addition, you are always in the practice of asking questions. You are documenting everything you learn, you are clear on the responsibilities you've taken ownership of, and take responsibility for your actions and inactions. Along the way, you have documented every accomplishment and opportunity for growth, ensuring that your setbacks and failures have fueled your imminent success.

Now, you're ready to take on more, to start your mentorship, embark on those learning opportunities which you negotiated when you were hired, all according to your agreed-upon timelines. Then you reach out to discuss the next steps. What if they then stall, make excuses, and sideline you? Perhaps they explain, because of certain unplanned circumstances, they're temporarily going to have to re-prioritize this. They promise to revisit this matter soon.

If you agree to or accept this, you are responsible for that choice and for allowing them to strip that power from you. You must take ownership of your response and responsibility for the results of your actions. Give them permission to offer you empty promises with nothing clear or tangible to go on, and you've fallen into the trappings of a carrot and stick career progression. Afterwards, you may find no way out from under their thumb.

This should constitute a clear break of contract. Trust is then also broken. Just as you are responsible for your own decisions and actions, they should likewise be accountable for their integrity and what they've promised. So, how do you navigate situations like this when they arise?

Luckily, there is a surefire way to further help your goals while increasing your worth. This following technique often results in their tactic backfiring spectacularly, while passively forcing their hand to give you what you want. It's simple... *Hold them accountable.* Make them answerable to their commitments.

Your role is crucial for the organization's success. Additionally, as a stakeholder, you consistently align your interests with what stands to benefit the organization. This makes it difficult for them to deny you what you are requesting. So, how to do this? Start by asking questions.

They've just told you something came up and they can't give you what you've negotiated—mentorship, pay, time off, title, remote work, etcetera. So, you ask questions.

✦What came up?

✦What else is being re-prioritized, and why?

✦How many of the organization's objectives were impacted?

✦What's the current focus, and how can I contribute to getting things back on track?

✦Are you expecting another delay?

✦How common is it when such obstacles arise?

✦How can we expand our focus so that important projects don't need to be shelved every time such a contingency arises?

✦You can count on me. What can I do to help the company maintain its priorities when such obstacles arise?

✦Let's set a flexible date range to reschedule our meeting. In the meantime, let's also set some dates for some monthly reviews where I can discuss with you everything I have accomplished when it comes to prioritizing the needs of our teams and organization, supplemented by a self-evaluation, and we can discuss my self-perception, and any advice and growth opportunities between now and our meeting.

✦We agreed when I was hired that my mentorship would begin by now. Can we set a new date in the coming weeks?

✦ How can I assist to ensure everyone can meet that goal?

Using these techniques instantly increases your worth, which continues to increase in value the longer they postpone your opportunities. The key is to appear sincere and show interest in growing with the organization to achieve your mutual goals. *This is a professional relationship.* And an arrangement has been reached.

Never let them shelf your needs to further their own goals, nor allow them to expect you to sacrifice your needs for nothing in exchange. This organization is not your child, nor are you the giving tree. You are *both* expected to profit from this arrangement. The second it becomes unprofitable for you is the second it is time to re-examine that relationship.

FOOL ME ONCE... FOOL ME TWICE...

The moment you get the feeling they might not live up to their end of the bargain, it's worth examining your future with them. And it's important to never grow comfortable or complacent with the velvet handcuffs they offer. The second you do that, you'll be taken advantage of while your professional worth decreases, eventually reaching the point where you're disposable. Do not let them strip you of your power. The only person you can trust and rely on is you. It is up to you to continue to advocate for higher pay, or to negotiate other factors that will increase your perceived professional worth in the industry.

So, just as you might read the morning paper or read your company's blog, you should also explore other companies whose values and accomplishments align with yours. Take up job hunting as a hobby. You'll never discover what better opportunities are out there without looking for them. Always keep your finger on the pulse of your industry and your worth. And remain loyal to your current employer, fully prepared to exit when it comes time to jump ship.

If it seems clear that they aren't going to live up to their word, tell them you are looking elsewhere. Make it clear you are focussed on your career, that you are still a bridge builder, and remind them you expressed from the onset what you were seeking in an employer, including your commitment to finding the right fit while advancing your career with a company that rewards your loyalty. Explain you were honest with what they can expect from you. Explain that you are ready to stay on board if they can make good on their promises without delay, but that you cannot delay your career progression any longer.

Don't hastily quit and put yourself in a compromised position, either. Rather, explore your prospects and talk to a head hunter and get their opinion of what you are worth. Compile some numbers and be prepared to seize opportunity when it presents itself.

Now, hopefully it won't come to this, and you'll find your dream job and successfully advocate for yourself. But if that doesn't unfold, increase your worth by building bridges, even if that means informing them you are giving them open notice and plan on looking for the right opportunity elsewhere. Inform them that you will take your time. If they'd like, you can even begin training your successor. Explain that you want everyone to land on their feet when you leave. That way, you can use this as an advertising point in your next round of interviews, which will increase your perceived value and professional worth.

In the final chapter of this book, we'll tie all of these principles together and how they all collectively quantify your professional worth. We'll also discuss how to address every angle to building on that worth, and how to get the most out of your efforts through salary, title, and anything that increases your value within your company, and across your industry or field.

Chapter 9
Commanding Your
Professional Worth

lthough it's more rare than common,
sometimes when a business goes through a
major restructure or rebranding, it's a sign
they're not doing well. And when this is true,
everyone's job is actually at risk. So how do you know?

By examining all their key performance indicators. By
understanding how the business looks on paper. You
can then ask whether this restructure or rebranding was
sudden, or planned out for years. How do the numbers
look? Are their accounts right-side up or up-side down?
We're talking about profits generated, how strong their

stocks are performing, how hard the executive branch is working, or how many hats the CEO is wearing.

When you see a business owner doing everything, from covering their staff's shifts and performing work below their pay grade, this could be a sign of a bigger problem. Which looks better on your resume? Do you go down with the ship? Or... Do you grab a life raft and preserve your career?

Sticking around till the end may reflect loyalty, but it's definitely not an indicator of success. It might imply you had few other prospects. When past performance is used as a predictor of future job performance, they also might assume you are okay going for weeks without pay. They might wonder how far you would selflessly sacrifice for them. Maybe they could use someone like you, someone who they can take advantage of.

You'll want to prioritize your career and be selfish, no matter how much you love the CEO or the idea of the company. Look after yourself. You are the only one you can count on to look after your best interests.

YOUR FIRST LOYALTY IS TO YOURSELF

Loyalty is greatly valued. This is a fact. And no doubt your loyalty and contributions have been recognized because you have gone to lengths to secure their deserved recognition. You also have a strong sense of what you have delivered, how you've helped their bottom line, and now have a deeper knowledge of the inner workings of the business than most of your peers. This, when it comes to performance reviews, makes you dreadful. This is the rare occasion where it is absolutely acceptable to make your employer's job more difficult.

They have to crunch numbers and justify how much they are paying who, the kind of pay increases their budget can afford, and how they will justify distributing increases fairly, based on merit, across their staff. This is where pay transparency is desirable. For example, when it merits paying a woman more than the other women they work with, that might be fair and equitable. However, if they are then being paid less than a man who performs a fraction of the work that woman does, that is unacceptable. In which case, the company might end up facing the choice of whether it would be more costly to replace them than to pay them their worth.

Sure, you may have proven your loyalty to your employer, but always be more loyal to yourself. Start by asking what your loyalty is worth and what that loyalty could cost your career advancement. Ask, will the growth you would see with your current employer increase your worth more than leaping into another opportunity elsewhere?

STRATEGIZE

Last chapter, we went through some of the dirty tricks and techniques frequently employed to weasel out of giving you the raise you deserve. With an understanding of the inner workings of the business, you'll be better equipped to anticipate and undermine every excuse they might offer to postpone your performance review or raise. Especially when meeting with them ahead of reviews, asking all the right questions, having a clear view of the big picture, or turning in an undeniable self-evaluation of everything you've done for the organization since your last review.

Specify in your self-evaluation the growth opportunities you've overcome. Provide a breakdown of the milestones you have surpassed and the goals you have achieved, whether for yourself or for the organization. Detail what you've done for them, for your teams, and quantify it with testimonials, facts, data, and numbers.

Steal their platform and don't give them a leg to stand on. Go in with a realistic understanding of what's behind the scenes. Factor in your knowledge of the range of what they can afford, and frame your asking price with consideration of that range. Showcase that you are prepared to outshine yourself and are ready to drive their success for the next quarter or annual plan. Doing so showcases even greater loyalty and keeps increasing your professional worth. You are basically saying that you are thinking in the best interests of the organization, which in turn makes it in their best interest to award you your fair asking price.

If they lowball you, give them a counteroffer. If you missed something and the number they return with is fair, considering an unforeseen factor, propose something supplemental. A company car. That corner office. Remote work. Anything reasonable that reduces your cost of living has a dollar value.

Yes, money matters, but always be thinking forward. More money right now is ideal. But how can you increase your worth in your industry? For example, a better title which may increase your visibility to headhunters. In fact, why not consult a headhunter for their insight on your market value? Can they offer you something that your current employer cannot? What does it hurt to put out your feelers and ask? Look at it as a fact-finding mission. Always keep your eye on the big picture of the long-game of your career.

PROJECTING YOUR INVESTMENT VALUE

Threatening to leave or take your skills and offerings elsewhere will only result in burning bridges or convincing them you were only ever in it for the money. Whereas showing how driven you are to advance your career, preferably with them, shows that you are looking to build bridges together. The more instrumental you are in supporting your team, through coaching or mentoring, the more a member of their family you'll be. Your determination, ability to learn from your mistakes, to grow, and your interest in furthering your mutual goals shows that you care. These always improve your positioning.

When you are rising up as a stakeholder—as an acting partner—you'll learn the company's budget and what they can afford. To incentivize them to pay you more, you need to increase their profit margin. When helping them reach their goals and adopting those goals as your own, you grow together. When it comes to increasing profits, they need someone reliable.

Are you a leader? We all are, to some degree. Maybe you're not commander supreme. Maybe you make a smaller impact than those in leadership positions. However, the key is being recognized for what you offer, and never allowing yourself to be marginalized. You are the commander of your career mission. Collect the data and witness for yourself what you are worth. Understand how their big picture compares to yours and how the two align.

So, when it comes to negotiating your pay raise, it is very similar to negotiating a salary. You first have to decide whether this opportunity is right for you. And everything that lowers your cost of living is negotiable-benefits, incentives, bonuses, perks, pay, etcetera.

How do you substantiate your worth? As we discussed, it all boils down to looking at *your* professional worth–industry recognition, competing offers, headhunter feelers, your accomplishments, what you anticipate bringing in for the company in the coming year–and putting a dollar value on those.

What if they explain they are restricting their payroll budget this round to funnel funds into some coming projects next quarter, which has the promise of increasing their payroll budget? *"So hang on, you'll get more next year."* This ploy isn't that uncommon. An appropriate response would be:

✦ *"Wow, that sounds great. I'm very interested in learning more about the conditions that led to this decision. So, what are we talking about here? Are you saying my pay increase next year will be what I should've gotten this year, combined with my projected pay increase next review period, plus an additional incentive for bypassing being rewarded for my efforts this round? Will this be provided in writing, with firm dates, regardless of whether those goals are met?"*

THE BIG PICTURE OF SUSTAINING A REALISTIC CAREER PROJECTION

Let's say that you've taken the advice offered in this book. You've personalized your systems approach, and are a rising star in the industry. You're having a great year, and you've never been happier. You won that promotion. You've been traveling for work and landed several big new accounts that were game changers for your organization. There's talk of a big fat bonus at year's end, and you decide it's time to buy a new car, buy a new house, and take that extravagant vacation you've been longing for. You rack up a bunch of credit card debt, spending money you don't yet have.

Then, the organization loses a key partner. A major account which that partner brought in jumps ship. Stock values plummet, and the organization has to re-evaluate everything. They announce budget cuts. They want to avoid laying off anyone and apologize that there will be no bonuses, and pay increases will be more modest than they had hoped.

Suddenly you feel like you are in a bind, and you justify that somehow the company is responsible for assuring you good times were to come. But your choices were your own, and the financial decisions you made weren't conducive to running your personal life like a business. Next, you find yourself pushing too hard for a raise because *you* need the money, and you're no longer thinking about the *business,* or how your needs *align.* Thus, your professional worth is in decline simply from losing sight of the mentality it takes to rise up.

While advancing your career, only live a lifestyle according to what you could afford prior to your last advancement. Always live within your means. Many people think that simply because they can afford a bigger apartment, they've stepped up. But every upgrade increases your cost of living and compromises your quality of life. Instead, comfortably preserve your work-life balance. Doing so will preserve what you offer as a professional.

Your problems are not theirs. But, throughout your professional relationship, their problems are yours. If you question whether that's fair, remember, they are paying you, not the other way around. The greater your control over your own life, the more calm and collected you'll be. The more confident, grounded, and centered you'll be, the greater your worth when they need you most.

But, decide whether it is worth sticking with them. If you truly have a scope of the big picture, and the data says that your efforts could pay off in turning the company around, you'll be a future partner, metaphorically or literally. However, if it's a sinking ship, do everything you can to help them, and get organized and ready to make a career move. Give them open notice of your plans to leave, and offer to train your successor to provide them a smooth transition while increasing their chances of success. This will increase your professional worth outside of the organization and within. Keeping the doors open will make it easy to rejoin their organization when they rebound. At the very least, you'll earn powerful references and glowing letters of recommendation.

Be honest with yourself regarding what your motivators are. Be selective when it comes to entering into a professional relationship. If you are primarily motivated by money, be honest with yourself, and inform your employer you are motivated by what working with them could do for your career in the long term. What are you pursuing? Title, which holds recruiter appeal? Are you interested in increased responsibility and more stake in your company? Are you hoping to get stock options, or industry recognition?

Maintain a work-life balance, living within your means, and only upgrade your lifestyle when it translates to ensuring continually secure financial standing and comfort. The greater your quality of life, and the stronger your disciplined habits are, the more confident you'll be.

When you walk the walk, it will be a power strut. When you talk the talk, you'll be able to talk circles around everyone around you. You'll speak in terms everyone understands, and know complex subject matter like the back of an expert's hand.

Most importantly, you'll have stored up your power simply by using common sense approaches to empowering yourself. You'll have the freedom to walk away from any job opportunity. Only you can make those decisions that are in your best interests. You'll preserve your dignity, self-respect, your psyche, and the power of being able to pick and choose from a long line of recruiters. And they'll all be lining up, competing to hire you, one of the most attractive professionals in your field.

This is what it means to be in command of your professional worth. It means commanding respect, acknowledgement, and being rewarded in equal measure to your merits.

Afterword
You Are The Writer of Your Story

Who are you? Are you prepared to do what is necessary to reach your destination? All it takes is creating a data bank of everything you offer, everything you stand for, and to create an attainable and easily definable professional model for driving your career where you want it to go. These are all just habits. You're planning ahead and writing everything down. You're scheduling time for work, for you, and for everything in between. You are setting boundaries, believing in yourself, and advocating for your worth.

Believe in no one more than believing in yourself!

You are asking questions, questioning authority, and mastering communication like never before. You are making friends, allies, and building bridges. You are becoming known in your community, and in your industry, which is smaller than you think. You are increasing your quality of life. And your increasing skills will enhance and benefit your life in every way.

Next time someone who you are in an intimate relationship with has an emotional outburst, and starts pointing fingers at something you did, you may find yourself responding non-defensively. You may end up breaking down the situation while keeping your cortisol levels in check. You might end up defusing that conflict before it escalates and find yourself in the leadership position of that relationship. Once you put everything in this book into practice, you'll discover you're in complete control of every controllable aspect of your life. And only you can answer what that is worth.